"The FrameWorks developed by Dennis Cheesebrow have been instrumental in my work with school boards, administrators, and community groups. Partnership; Redefined captures the essence of Dennis' work and practices as a coach and consultant. The FrameWorks have developed my capacity to build true partnerships with teachers, administrators, school boards, and community groups."

Sue Ann Gruver, Ph.D.
Superintendent, Prior Lake– - Savage Public Schools

"Creating mutually beneficial and mutually satisfying partnerships is a real skill - one that requires understanding of the motivations, needs, and communication styles of the people engaged in partnership. In this book, Dennis Cheesebrow looks at the fundamentals of partnership and offers a variety of perspectives, including that of personality, as a means of creating cooperative and collaborative partnerships. Partnerships where all involved feel heard and appreciated for what they each bring to the team."

Carol Ritberger, Ph.D.
Author of " What Color is Your Personality? Red, Orange, Yellow or Green" and "Managing People ... What's Personality Got To Do With It?"

Dennis Cheesebrow is the sage trusted by the best school PR professionals I know. I can't imagine navigating a critical organizational change issue without knowing, "What does Dennis think?"

Colin Sokolowski,
Director of Public Relations, Mounds View Public Schools
Author of "The Accidental Adult"

"I have experienced the frustration of working in organizations with low trust and isolation that make it difficult to accomplish a shared mission. The FrameWorks developed in Partnership Redefined have become a primary resource for my work in building the partnerships needed to drive shared commitment to goals. Cheesebrow's FrameWorks help leaders develop new ways to think about the work of mission-driven organizations."

Larry Leverett, Ph.D.
Executive Director,
Panasonic Foundation

"The term partnership evokes compelling images of interdependent cultures that support high performance and valued outcomes. But situated in organizational hierarchy, what does partnership look like and how is it grown? In Partnership: Redefined, Dennis Cheesebrow offers a set of tools and processes, refined through years of use with varied organizations, to guide leaders in their work to optimize human and social potential for the good of organizations in service to their communities.

Jennifer York-Barr, Ph.D. , Professor of Organizational
Leadership, Policy, and Development Academy of Distinguished
Teachers, University of Minnesota

"Once again Cheesebrow proves to be a master of the inner workings of organizations. In his accessible style he provides practical FrameWorks for promoting healthy and productive work cultures."

Rick Spicuzza, Ph.D.
Assistant Superintendent of Curriculum and Assessment
South Washington County., School District. 833

Printed in the United States of America

First Printing, 2012

ISBN: 978-0-9856550-0-6

property of Bogman Publishing, LLC

Dennis Cheesebrow, TeamWorks International Inc.

7037 20th Ave. S.

Centerville, MN 55038

www.partnershipredefined.com

Dedicated to

Bonnie

One true Partnering soul, spirit, and sage

with whom I have learned, loved, and lived real partnership;

my deepest gratitude, amazement and love.

Foreword

A book about partnership requires a myriad of good and talented people who have supported, challenged, affirmed, and even doubted, at times, the approach and "stretch" that partnership asks of individuals and organizations. This "stretching" has also been a source of development and support for me as well over the years. I am deeply grateful for my mentors and supporters along the way.

Mentors and teachers from whom I have learned so much:

Bob Collopy	John Flannigan	Kathleen Joyce
Virginia Pierce	Mirja Hanson	Duncan Toll
Jim Lundholm-Eades	Fr. Kevin McDonough	Ginny Belden-Charles
Marcia Hyatt	Sr. Fran Donnelly	John Cherek
Tim Cheesebrow	John Cheesebrow	Paul Cheesebrow

Respected colleagues who provided feedback, challenge, and support :

Ric Dressen	Karen Orcut	Christine Wroblewski
Jennifer York-Barr	Jim Lundholm-Eades	Rick Spicuzza
Larry Leverett	Marcia Hyatt	Glenda Eoyang
Dan Hoverman	Chace Anderson	Colin Sokolowski
Jay Haugen	Jeff Ronneberg	Ginny Belden-Charles

The "Team" at TeamWorks International

Julie, Bonnie, Rich, Matt, Tim, and Connie

This is a book about partnership, redefined as a capacity of human organizations and not limited to individuals or to managers. This is a book with real tools that work, honed for over two decades in a wide variety of organizations and settings across diverse markets and organizations: public and private education, human services providers, faith-based institutions and dioceses, parishes, congregations and churches, city, county and state government agencies, nonprofit organizations, small businesses and corporations.

Partnership: Redefined is designed for use by everyone in an organization. However, it is written in language and with examples that speak more directly to those who manage and lead. Partnership requires an intentional choice by those who lead an organization to develop the culture and practices of partnership. Partnership has to provide mission-level and operational benefits to organizations and individuals that are demonstrable, make sense, and feel right. For most leaders I have worked with, partnership capacity development is a strategic choice to accomplish mission, vision, and performance targets.

Partnership: Redefined may be, for some, a challenge to current models of leadership. Many of these models are rich in story and offer compelling language about leadership, but the focus is the individual. In Partnership: Redefined, leadership is defined as a capacity and action of all, and management is a capacity and action of those with delegated authority to do so. Thus leadership is a true shared capacity rather than the reserved capacity of management.

The resulting philosophy is "Partner When WE Should & Manage When I Must."

In addition, I provide tools and processes for this shared leadership capacity called partnership. These tools and processes are called FrameWorks™ and you will hear real stories about real applications. The FrameWorks are leadership action tools for all, not reserved for a few.

Partnership is a key for unleashing the latent creativity and ownership that remains largely untapped in most organizations, and it is a strategy for reducing stress and increasing performance at the same time. Partnership can be a challenge and sometimes a threat for those leaders with high ego and self-absorption who assume employees are less trustworthy and competent than themselves. I have had some client engagements where partnership stood as a clear challenge to the power systems at play in the organization. A few asked me to leave. However, partnership is also an opportunity for learning and transformation. And many clients have asked me to stay and work at building a new way of seeing, working, relating, and performing. For those opportunities of learning and growth I have been and am deeply grateful.

The chapters of the book are organized around the fundamental work of most organizations and what I have observed as some of the foundational patterns of work and relationships.

Introduction:
Partnership: A Different Way of Thinking, Working, and Leading

Throughout the book, I will state and restate that partnership is not natural or easy for most leaders and organizations. In the Introduction, I provide observations about typical patterns of organizational life I have experienced and explored. A redefinition of partnership and its relationship to and differences from power-based approaches are provided with real examples and reflection. The definition and importance of FrameWorks to the capacity development of partnership is detailed, and key understandings of partnership development are provided for reflection, as well as some important challenges and benefits for its investment.

Chapter One: Building Trust

Trust is a foundational element for all groups and organizations committed to partnership. Building and managing trust is a critical skill and responsibility of leadership. The Leadership Choices FrameWork is introduced as an effective tool for real-time assessment of trust-mistrust. It describes the differences between the states of partnership and isolation. In addition, a simple process for using the Leadership Choices FrameWork is provided for immediate application to your daily work.

Chapter Two: Guiding Change

"Managing change" is a well-worn phrase and challenge for most organizations. One reason is because "change" is present in every organization, every day. And it's not going away anytime soon. A basic skill of leadership is guiding change without being in the room—leadership in absence rather than presence. Doing so requires the ability to build trust and competence in others. The Guiding Change FrameWork is introduced as a practical tool that many find useable immediately. I see Guiding Change as the "training wheels" on the first Partnership bike one rides. It's a proven and reliable way to begin developing the partnership capacity in oneself and the organization. Compelling stories and examples provide an instant understanding and feel for how to use this partnership process.

Chapter Three: Seeing Authority and Power

Authority and power is found in all organizations. Much of my thinking in this area is grounded in the work of Barry Oshry, author of Seeing Systems II, In the Middle and The Organizational Workshop (TOPS, MIDDLES, BOTTOMS and CUSTOMERS), among many other incredibly useful approaches and tools in organizational development. I introduce the Authority and Power FrameWork as a useful reflection and strategy tool for individuals and groups in managing three types of "capital." This FrameWork is a tool for leaders in managing the environment and risks of an organization so that partnership can flourish and performance can improve.

Chapter Four: Managing Transitions

Every change in an organization causes change for every employee in an organization. Many organizations assume that employees can manage personal and professional transitions as easy as waking up in the morning. But that is not my experience with thousands of employees in hundreds of organizations, nor with myself. The Transition and Change FrameWork is an easy and effective tool for assessing transitions, learning, professional development, and performance management. It can be applied at the individual, group, or organizational level. If Guiding Change is like training wheels for partnership capacity development, then Transition and Change is the bike itself. It will take an organization to deeper clarity, dialogue, and choice making about the personal and professional development so needed in all organizations.

Chapter Five: Making Decisions

Decision making is a fundamental process of organizational life, one that's often not mapped nor defined but wrapped in layers of positional authority and power assumptions. The Decision Making FrameWork is introduced as a proven tool for public and private settings across business, public education, and faith-based organizations. It helps differentiate roles, responsibilities, and relationships in a way that builds partnership. The traps and myths of "consensus-building" are explored and practical applications are described. The chapter explores the five steps of decision making and introduces choice making as a step in that process. It describes how to include stakeholders in a practical and effective way, not as "due diligence," but as a critical part of the process. The Decision Making FrameWork includes the critical steps of implementation and refinement as part of a continuous improvement loop.

Chapter Six: Leveraging the Strengths of Personality

In the typical "problem-solving" culture of most organizations, little attention is given to individual and group strengths. One can't use gap analysis without defining what's real and present. The Four Color View FrameWork applies the work of Carol Ritberger's Color Personality Indicator® to the individual, group, and organization. Four personality types (Red, Green, Orange, and Yellow) are evaluated in light of strengths, wants, and preferences, and are applied to communication, processing, and decision-making. Applications are provided for using each personality type to build partnership.

Conclusion: Intentional Choice

Here I summarize my learning about developing partnership capacity with individuals, groups, and organizations—both the benefits and the challenges. I offer tips for those exploring the possibilities of partnership.

And at the end I take a moment to explore how partnership and porcupines go together. But don't turn to that page yet. Read the book first.

Partnership: Redefined
Leadership Through the Power of **&**

Dennis Cheesebrow

Contents

Partnership : Redefined

Introduction:

Partnership:
A Different Way of Thinking, Working, and Leading

Ever had this happen?

You're one of a half dozen people in the office who have gathered to talk about a report that's due in two days. You've been exchanging emails for the last week, but today it seems like an informal meeting is in order. Somebody else is using the conference room, so your group decides to assemble in the lounge. Ten minutes into the meeting, the boss pops in to get a cup of coffee. Suddenly, everyone looks up and the room goes quiet.

What do you feel?

It's definitely not guilt. The conversation, although free-ranging, was task-oriented. Still, the boss's unannounced presence made things awkward. It's not as though she said something to make people feel that way. In fact, she didn't say anything at all—just nodded, got her coffee, and left.

So what's going on here?

You and your colleagues ran smack up against hierarchy, against authority, against power. That power wasn't verbalized or expressed in any overt way, but it became part of the room's atmosphere, and it temporarily squelched the spirit of collegiality and mutuality that everyone had been enjoying. When the boss left, that collegial spirit quickly re-emerged and everyone picked up where they'd left off.

But what if the boss had stuck around? Even if she just listened in, things probably would have been different—less joking, more buzz words, maybe a sudden attempt to make it seem like you were following an agenda, perhaps a collective effort to appear more "professional." People would have been more likely to wait for her initiative and perhaps more cautious in advancing their own ideas and more deferential in responding to others. They would have fallen into predictable patterns of working and relating—probably without even being aware they were doing so.

And if you're the boss, how do you feel? What's it like to walk into a room and have everyone clam up, then hear conversation pick up again as you're walking down the hall?

Although subordinates might imagine they'd enjoy exercising the power that can quiet a room without saying a word, most leaders I talk to don't relish those situations at all. "I wish they'd just be themselves and keep working," is what I hear them say.

Hierarchy: A Fact of Life

Hierarchy and difference is one of the ways people organize themselves. It's good and works well in many settings, cultures, and organizations. When I was a kid and we would choose sides to play softball, one of the first questions to emerge was, "Who's the captain?" followed closely by, "How come I'm not the captain?" and, "When will I get picked?"

That's not because some adult told us that you can't play softball without captains. It's because, based on our observations, experience, and instincts, we figured out that having someone decide who's going to play where and what the batting order will be made the game run more smoothly than if all those decisions had to be negotiated.

But although most of us recognize the value of hierarchy, we also sense and experience its limitations. We know, whether we're conscious of it at any given moment or not, that relationships governed largely by differences in power and authority can lock people into roles and behaviors that stifle creativity and thwart innovation. We know that a complete absence of hierarchy is unproductive, but we also know that an automatic deferral to defined roles isn't always the best course of action.

What are we looking for?

A Complement to Hierarchy: Partnership

People who have thought a lot about this dynamic have come up with a variety of ways to describe it. In the educational realm, psychologist Lev Vygotsky called the optimal learning environment for a child "the zone of proximal development." Learning flourishes, Vygotsky believed, when children have recourse to adult assistance as they need it but when they also enjoy the freedom to engage in individual and group problem solving on their own—to test their own capacity for learning.

What's true for children turns out to be true for adults as well. For example, Ron Tinsley and Kimberly Lebak used Vygotsky's notion to explore what they called the "zone of reflective capacity," the ability of adults to expand their capacity for reflection when they collaborate with others who have similar goals. Tinsley and Lebak found that sharing feedback and analysis and evaluating each other's work increased people's ability to engage in critical reflection. The zone of reflective capacity enlarged as people's trust and understanding of each other grew.

All of us function best when we have a mix of freedom and support. I've found that complete freedom is rarely productive for organizations and individuals. One word to describe such a state of affairs in the workplace is chaos. Chaos reigns when the number of variables being dealt with is high and the predictability of outcomes is low. Chaos might leave people feeling free to do whatever they want, but it's also likely to leave them feeling unconnected, and unmoored.

The opposite of chaos is control. Control reigns when the number of variables being dealt with is low and the predictability of outcome is high. Control might leave people feeling safe and comfortable, but it's also likely to leave them feeling stifled and limited.

Figure 1

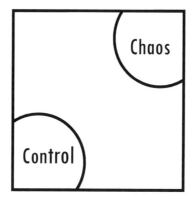

Between chaos and control is an area where human inventiveness, creativity, productivity, and ownership flourish. It's an area where people are free to act individually or collectively as the situation warrants. It's an area where leaders and subordinates operate proactively and collegially rather than reactively and competitively. I call this area the zone of partnership. Partnership reigns when the number of variables being dealt with is moderate and the predictability of outcome is moderate.

Figure 2

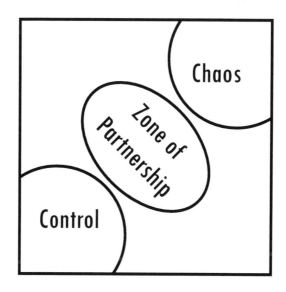

Organizations do not permanently exist in any one of these states but usually oscillate among them, sometimes by coincidence and sometimes by choice. When I'm first asked to engage with an organization, it's typical for the organization to be oscillating between chaos and control, looking for a magic solution from the outside that will lead to calm, control, and success. Rarely do leaders see the zone of partnership as a strategy or a capacity of the organization.

Partnership: A Way of Relating, Living, and Working

People form partnerships in many areas of life. Marriage, for example, is a partnership with several potential dimensions: economic, social, sexual, parental. The institution of marriage has varied across time and cultures, and even in contemporary American society there is a range of marital relationships and behavior that most people recognize as valid.

For instance, a partner who gets married might choose to adopt the other partner's surname or keep one's own. A couple with different last names is no less married than one with the same last name.

Similarly, a married couple might choose to maintain separate checking accounts or to establish a joint account. A couple with separate accounts is no less married than one with a joint account.

At any given time, both members of a marriage might choose to work full-time outside the home, or one might choose to work at home raising a child, or they might both decide to cut their hours to facilitate child-rearing. As parents, they might attempt to share roles and responsibilities equally, or they might agree to adopt some kind of division of labor.

Partnership recognizes that people have different stories, talents, and gifts. Partnership recognizes and respects the differences in authority and power, but it does not blindly defer to lines of authority. Partnership is less concerned with defining individuals as equals and more concerned that people are able to contribute to the collective good in ways that maximize their abilities.

Partnership does not mean obliterating hierarchy or ignoring differences in authority or power. It does not mean people are accountable to no one but themselves, nor does it necessarily mean majority rule.

Partnership does mean a mutual decision to suspend authority and hierarchy, to interact as peers who are committed to making each other and the organization successful. It does mean suspending one's own need to control a situation. It does mean assuming that others are worthy of trust and can be relied on to carry their own weight for the good of the whole.

Partnership empowers all participants to contribute to an organization based on their unique strengths and perspectives. It does so by enabling people at different levels of power and authority to entrust their self-interests to each other to accomplish shared goals. Partnership means a mutual acceptance of responsibility and ownership. It means using all of an organization's resources—human, material, institutional—with interdependence and service.

Barry Oshry describes partnership as "a relationship in which we are jointly committed to the success of whatever endeavor, process, or project we are engaged in." Partnership for Oshry is reciprocal. It means "being a person who sees others—who grasps why they are and what is important to them, who gets behind them and helps move them ahead in their world, as well as being a person who puts your projects out to others—who lets them know who you are and what is important to you, who allows them to get behind you and move you ahead in your world."

As a relationship, partnership contains the people, the connections, and the space between them. These three dynamics are important to recognize and steward in an ongoing and intentional manner by all involved.

Partnership both constrains and enlivens people's behavior. In partnership, leaders are less apt to use their authority and power to impose their ideas and solutions on followers. In partnership, followers are less apt to leave the responsibility for organizational success entirely in the hands of leaders. Partnership creates a sense of shared work and mutual commitment. It binds people together in a common purpose and relationship.

Partnership, as I've said, exists between the states of chaos and control. It's an alternative to hierarchy. In partnership, people agree to set aside what might be traditional ways of relating. But partnership is not only a form of interpersonal relationships and it isn't primarily based on liking others or being interested in similar pursuits. Partnership is professional. It's an organizational culture and practice that is developed and supported in a strategic manner because there is an operational purpose and payoff for its presence.

Many might initially see partnership as "soft" and management as "hard." That's not the case. Partnership is a shared and effective leadership capacity and practice of the people in an organization. I have seen, heard, and felt it when:

- Parents, teachers, administrators, and school board members are in a discussion, grounded in data and personal stories about the intersection of learning, race, gender, and poverty and what the community can do about it.

- Employees and managers, from the manufacturing floor to the executive suite, are around a table deep in conversation about shared sacrifice in order to keep a small business afloat in tough economic conditions.

- Parishioners, ministry directors, and pastors go through days of dialogue and planning about a pastoral plan to revitalize their faith community in times of pain, distrust, and fear.

- Physicians, experts, and state health officials work to create an effective and ethical process for distributing scarce hospital resources during a pandemic outbreak or terrorist or nuclear event. What do you do when there is not enough for all and many will die while some will live?

Partnership: A Different Way of Organizing

The very term organization indicates that when people band together to accomplish something, they need a way of structuring or organizing themselves. Traditionally, that's been done in three ways.

One model is hierarchical. Oshry distinguishes among "Tops, who have overall responsibility for the organization; Bottoms, who do the work of the organization; and Middles, who administer, manage, or supervise the work of others." When a course of action must be determined, the organization appeals to the Top, to the leader's authority. The assumption is that good leaders will make good decisions.

A second model is institutional. Here, authority might still be hierarchical but is also vested in policies and procedures. People still occupy different roles in the organization, but when confronted with a decision, the organization appeals, not necessarily to a designated person, but to an agreed-upon policy. Examples of institutions are state and federal government agencies and many traditional religious denominations. The assumption is that good laws, policies, and procedures lead to good decisions.

Another common model is collaborative. Typically, in collaborative organizations people are organized into teams. Team members have similar status and decision making follows discussion in which all contributions are heard, honored, and discussed. The assumption is that good groups and group dynamics lead to good decisions.

Hierarchical, institutional, and collaborative structures are not mutually exclusive. Many large organizations operate with some aspects of all three: There are managers, there is a manual of operations, and there are work teams. But most organizations don't have an integrated way of coordinating those entities, and the employees might not even recognize that there are distinctive and not always compatible models of organizational structure at work.

Furthermore, what works reasonably well during normal conditions might not work when the organization faces a challenge or crisis. Under such conditions, it might appear easiest to defer to a command-control version of hierarchical leadership (let the boss decide) or to a narrow view of institutional authority (what does the manual say?). So, chaos gives way to control, a decision is made, and a the sense of crisis dissipates. What's often left, however, is a nagging sense of discontent and a feeling that there must be a better way.

Defining Partnership

There is a better way, and it's called partnership. Partnership is a different way of thinking, working, and leading. Partnership is dynamic, not static. Partnership emerges as a specific response to a specific situation. The roles that people assume in partnership change as conditions change. In short, one should expect partnership to look different next time than it did this time or last time.

Leadership is the combination of individual authority to manage and command, & the organizational capacity of partnership. The most effective leaders I know are able to "Partner When WE Should & Manage When I Must." These leaders spend as much as 70% of their time in partnership & only 30% in management.

Partnership requires effective management first. The trust to partner is built by managing fairly, consistently, and effectively—not the other way around. Otherwise, the act of partnership represents too much risk for those who produce in an organization.

Partnership is the subject of this book and is the cornerstone of the TeamWorks International approach to everything we do: strategic planning, leadership development, and managing change implementation.

FrameWorks™ as THE Partnership Capacity Tools

To help organizations develop their capacity for partnership, we use FrameWorks. FrameWorks are innovative and effective images, processes and tools that rely on the power of images to clarify and reframe problems, mediate authority differences, envision solutions, and implement change.

Images are critical to partnership as a mediator of relationships among those with differing authority and power in an organization. Without an image or graphic that belongs to the organization and not the individual, it is often the authority difference that mediates the relationship. Those with the most authority in an organization are generally the least aware of this reality, and those with the least authority are the most aware.

FrameWorks are effective images for the basic and critical work that occurs every day in all organizations. Throughout this book, I'll describe how FrameWorks can be applied to the everyday work of organizations. The overarching principle for all those examples and the context in which they take place is partnership.

Partnership is Real

Partnership is a tangible capacity that creates a cultural and performance change that one can see, hear, and experience. Partnership produces measurable results. Signs that partnership are operating in the workplace include the following:

- Shared accountability for the organization's mission, vision, and performance.

- Less ego and self-centeredness on the part of leaders, employees, and groups.

- More creativity, innovation, and ownership.

- Greater clarity of roles, responsibilities, and authority.

- Greater flexibility and nimbleness in responding to dynamic and shifting conditions.

- A shift from a problem- and deficit-based environment to an asset- and strength-based environment, a movement from scarcity to abundance.

If that's the kind of organization you want to work in and for, this book is for you.

Chapter 1:
Building Trust

Does this sound familiar?

Rick arrives at his office and checks his email. Here's the third message in his inbox:

From: Dave Crawford
Subject: Today's Meeting
Date: June 27, 2011 3:47:01 PM CST
To: Rick Edwards
Cc: TeamLeader@newsolutions.net, DVisionLeader@newsolutions.net, VPMarketing@newsolutions.net, VPCommunications@newsolutions.net, VPOperations@newsolutions.net, VPSales@newsolutions.net

....

Rick,
I'm following up on Friday's meeting. I hope that subsequent reports will make better use of the data you had to work with.

I'd also add that presentation software being what it is today, I would think that something other than bar graphs might be considered when presenting an important report. I don't think I need to remind you that your colleagues are busy people who expect meetings to be run smoothly and efficiently.

Dave Crawford
Operations Manager
New Solutions, Inc.

After reading the message, Rick is peeved. Then, he goes back and checks the Cc list. Now he's really steamed. He asks himself, What's the point of copying all these people? If Dave wants to chew me out for how I handled the meeting, that's one thing. But there's no reason to bring half the company in on it. And the thing is, I always thought, Dave and I had a good relationship. Now what am I supposed to think?

Doubting and Believing

Partnership is founded on trust, and there is no more serious threat to partnership than mistrust. Mistrust is a form of doubt. It arises when you question someone or something. For Rick, the seeds of doubt were sown by his perception of Dave's tone in the post-meeting email. "I thought he respected me; now I'm not sure." Those seeds were then watered by Rick's assumption about Dave's motives for deciding whom to copy on the message. "He's trying to make me look bad in front of everyone, including people who weren't at the meeting."

For some people, doubt is their default setting. Peter Elbow, a writing teacher, argues that our intellectual tradition has emphasized what he calls the "doubting game" over the "believing game." The purpose of the doubting game, says Elbow, is a valid one: to get at the truth. It starts with the assumption that in order to test the truth of an assertion, one must begin by doubting it. Only after passing the rigorous test of doubt will something reveal itself to be true.

The believing game, on the other hand, starts with the assumption that understanding something or someone is aided by belief more than by doubt. Believing can be difficult, Elbow acknowledges, when something seems absurd or contrary. Believing means "trying to get inside the head of someone who saw things this way," and that effort requires imagination and resolve.

Doubting, for Elbow, is not simply a reflection of personality. The doubting game has a long and distinguished tradition stretching back to Socrates and continuing with Descartes. Modern science, in the view of some, owes much of its success to an enlightened skepticism. Indeed, says Elbow, "some scientists talk as though they never really believe anything at all, but merely act as though certain things were true if they haven't yet been disproved." Playing the doubting game, then, is associated with being rational, disciplined, tough-minded. Those who play the believing game, on the other hand, can be seen as irrational, lazy, gullible.

By referring to these two dispositions—doubting and believing—as games, Elbow intends to emphasize several things. For starters, a game is not natural or inevitable; it's something invented, with rules that work well but that could be otherwise.

Some rules are perfectly arbitrary. If you run the bases clockwise in a baseball game, you'll be called out. But baseball would probably work just as well if players ran the bases clockwise rather than counterclockwise, as long as everyone agreed to that rule.

Other rules can't be changed without radically altering the game. If you eliminated the rule that a pitch is either a strike or a ball, batters would be free to wait for pitches that they like and a game would take much longer to play—as indeed it does in much sandlot baseball.

The doubting game has rules that most of us are familiar with: look before you leap; measure twice, cut once; don't trust anyone over/under 30; when in doubt, don't. The believing game might be less familiar, but it has rules too, and abiding by them is necessary to make the game work.

Another thing about games is that they're usually played with others. Both the doubting game and the believing game achieve their utility and power when those activities are shared with others, although the latter is more dependent on that sharing than is the former. "The function of a group in the believing game," says Elbow, "is for people to help each other believe more things, experience more things, and thereby move away from the lowest-common-denominator tendency in a majority conclusion."

Suppose you're in a meeting and four alternatives have been presented. Most people find 2 and 3 the easiest to believe and 4 the most difficult. But although you can see the value of 2 and 3, you find 4 the most believable. Playing the doubting game would mean trying to get the rest of the group to question 2 and 3. Playing the believing game means trying to help others see what you see in 4.

Elbow sees the doubting and believing games associated with particular attributes and behavior, both cognitive and affective:

Doubting Game	Believing Game
• extrication, disengagement	• involvement
• detachment, perspective	• projection, commitment
• resisting what is new	• willingness to explore what is new
• closing, clenching	• opening, loosening
• literal	• metaphorical
• rigid	• flexible
• stubborn, hanging on	• yielding
• impulse for securing	• impulse for risk
• centered, unmoving self	• floating self
• learning to be sharper, finer, more piercing, harder, tougher	• learning to be larger, more encompassing, softer, more absorbent
• aggressive: meeting threat by beating it down	• nonaggressive: meeting threat by bending, incorporating
• deflating	• supporting
• competitive	• cooperative
• solitary or adversary activity	• working in a group
• talking, noise, arguing	• listening, silence, agreeing
• defending my position	• asking you about your position

I've seen the doubting and believing game play out in meetings and conversations. Partnership needs both games, but often the doubting game appears easier for many people, while the believing game seems to require more effort. If the doubting game prevails in meetings and conversations, then mistrust is more likely to influence relationships and the work and decisions being made. If the believing game is more prevalent, then trust and confidence in self and others emerges more readily and influences the work and decisions being made.

1. When and with whom is it easier for you to play the doubting game?

2. When and with whom is it easier for you to play the believing game?

3. How would Dave's response have been different if he played the believing game?

4. How might choosing a believing response to those you tend to doubt bring about different consequences or results?

Choosing Trust

I've been talking about the doubting game and believing game in relation to statements and ideas, but they also apply to people. Rick's crisis resulted from doubts about his status in the company and his relationship to Dave. When you're playing the doubting game, it's an easy step to move from having doubts about a relationship to mistrusting the other person(s).

Opportunities for mistrust are numerous—emails like the one Rick received, angry phone calls, misunderstanding and miscommunication—and no workplace is immune from them. Indeed, "stuff" happens every day, and when it does, doubt and mistrust often follow in its wake. Our natural reaction to "stuff" is for doubt about others to rise and defensiveness to set in. Doubt and defensiveness lead to isolation and are often accompanied by a tendency to question the other person's competence.

To build trust and deal directly with doubt and mistrust, I use the Leadership Choices FrameWork. It's a reflection tool that requires one to pause and choose either partnership or isolation. I call this FrameWork Leadership Choices because by making a conscious choice to move toward trust in the face of doubt, one is performing an act of leadership that's grounded in partnership rather than hierarchy—and that choice is open to anyone. And in doing so, one is choosing to operate in the Zone of Partnership rather than Control or Chaos.

This FrameWork is based on my experience that partnership is not easy for many people and first requires raising our awareness about relationships, words, and actions. Partnership always involves awareness, intention, and choice on an ongoing, minute-by-minute basis. It is a conscious act, not a reflexive one.

Once one is aware of being in doubt about others' trust and competence, one makes a choice to operate in the isolation mode (right oval) or the partnership mode (left oval). And, that decision to operate in partnership is usually made in the midst of doubt, not in the absence of doubt.

Leadership Choices FrameWork

Figure 3

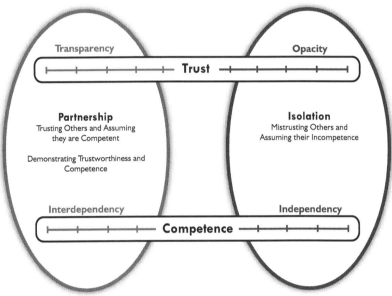

As this FrameWork illustrates, people work on a continuum with partnership at one end and isolation at the other. Based on my own observations about myself and others, when faced with stressful situations, people tend to move right on the continuum—away from partnership and toward isolation. That movement is accompanied by growing mistrust in others; a tendency to assume that others are not competent; a go-it-alone attitude (independency); and a determination not to reveal one's own knowledge, opinions, motives, or feelings (opacity). When people are operating in partnership, on the other hand, they choose to operate with trust in others and their competencies. Their attitudes and actions are motivated by a desire for and spirit of interdependence, openness, and transparency.

I want to emphasize that moving to the right on the partnership–isolation continuum doesn't mean one is a "bad" person. That movement simply reflects a typical unconscious response, and it's more likely to occur in times of stress or uncertainty, and when we feel challenged or threatened.

When "stuff" happens and doubt rises, most people naturally move to the right in an instant. Choosing to operate in partnership is just that—a choice, and one that requires reflection, intention, and sometimes courage. The goal is to operate intentionally rather than automatically, proactively rather reactively, with self-awareness rather than self-protection.

How can you do that?

One way to start is by asking some probing questions:

- What do I tend to assume about other people, and how do those assumptions affect my attitudes, actions, and decisions?

- What situations, events, or people tend to "hook" me, tempting me to move away from partnership, trust, and collaboration?

- How might my immediate reaction to a situation be different in a few minutes, hours, or days?

- What would happen if I took the time and deliberation to respond differently from the way I'm inclined to respond?

Taking Time

As I noted earlier, playing the believing game takes time. Because many of us may have been acculturated to play the doubting game, we've absorbed its rules and we play it instinctively. Doubting something takes little exertion.

The act of believing, on the other hand, usually requires effort and may involve investigating, listening, synthesizing, and deliberating. Resisting the tendency to react almost always takes more time than simply reacting would.

A commitment to partnership means resisting what Peter Elbow calls "the itch for closure" and embracing an attitude that Margaret Wheatley describes as "being comfortable with uncertainty." It demands patience and waiting. Elbow says that if "you need answers at the end of three months, spend the first 2½ months not-trying for them. If you have only an hour, spend the first 50 minutes not-looking for answers."

Consensus Caution

It might be assumed that when I emphasize the importance of taking time in a group I'm talking about achieving consensus. That may or may not be the case. For one thing, as Edwin Olson and Glenda Eoyang observe, consensus isn't necessarily the best goal for a group: "Too often, seeking consensus suppresses differences and generates solutions that lose the creativity and self-organizing potential of the group." Olson and Eoyang recommend amplifying differences by "unbraiding" them so that differences are recognized and valued.

If consensus is an ultimate goal, achieving it in a group of any size will take longer than for one person to make a unilateral decision, and organizations committed to operating by consensus must be prepared to wait before acting. Generally, groups without the authority to make a decision can reach consensus regarding the current reality and envisioned future, but rarely regarding specific strategic and tactical decisions—largely because they are not truly accountable for that level of choice making. But even when a leader will be the one making a decision, there is value in hearing others out, in considering alternatives, in playing the believing game. Operating in partnership doesn't always mean operating by consensus, but it does mean trusting others, assuming they're competent, and being willing to change one's mind.

Partnership: A Choice—of Sorts

In noting that partnership isn't our natural way of behaving and relating, I've emphasized that it's something we must choose. That's true in a sense, but from another perspective, partnership and all it involves—trusting others and assuming their competence—isn't a choice at all. The fact is, our lives depend on trusting others. Trust can be conscious or unconscious, and it can be serious or mundane.

Say you walk into a conference room where you've never been before and choose a chair to sit in. You probably don't begin by testing an available chair to be sure it will support you. You just sit down. In so doing, you're exercising an unconscious and mundane form of trust. You're assuming that the people who made the chair are competent, as are the people who chose these chairs for this room. It's possible that a given chair at your disposal is defective and will collapse or tip over when you sit on it, but you don't behave on the basis of that possibility.

Now let's put you behind the wheel of a car on a two-lane highway. When you meet an approaching vehicle, do you move to the shoulder in case the driver strays over the center line? No. You operate on the assumption that the other driver is competent. In so doing, you're exercising an unconscious form of trust, albeit one that's more consequential than that which governed your behavior with the chair. It's possible that a given driver, due to inattention or impairment, will cross the center line, but you don't behave on the basis of that possibility.

An example of conscious trust, and one with serious consequences, is dramatized in a recent film, Meek's Cutoff. In 1845, a small group of American settlers on the Oregon Trail has hired a mountain man, Stephen Meeks, to guide them through the Cascade Mountains. Meeks claims to know a shortcut, but a trip that was supposed to take two weeks has now taken five. Doubts about Meeks' competence and intentions arise. Does he know what he's talking about? Perhaps, someone speculates, he was hired to do away with would-be settlers in order to keep the wilderness pristine. Then the group encounters a lone Paiute Native American, whom they take hostage. With food and water running low, they must decide whether to follow Meeks or their hostage, whose language they can't understand but who, when given a chance to lead them, seems to know where he's going. Who would you choose to follow?

Most of us rarely face life-and-death decisions, but every day we do all sorts of things based on trust. I trust that the food I buy in a supermarket or restaurant won't make me sick. I trust that the water from the cooler in the staff lounge will be safe to drink. I trust that drivers will respect the white line that demarcates the lane I'm bicycling in. I trust that the bridge we're crossing will hold us up. I trust, I trust, I trust.

Trusting doesn't mean being naïve. It's good to drive defensively. You shouldn't eat or drink something that looks or smells funny. But to go through life mistrusting everyone and everything isn't an option. Complete independence and autonomy isn't an option.

If I'm committed to partnership—to working with others across the differences of authority and power, with the goal of developing innovation and ownership in my organization—then I must manage the daily dynamics of living amid differing degrees of doubt, of trust and mistrust, of competence and incompetence. My awareness of these dynamics and relational needs in the moment means I must make a choice: a leadership choice to operate either in isolation or partnership.

That continuing choice, of isolation or partnership, in the midst of doubt, creates the potential for an organization to innovate, to transform its culture, and to succeed. The choice is continual, but if I act consistently it can become a comfortable, if not predictable, one. Its impact is my accountability. The organization might just be needing, hoping, waiting for the right choice to be made. Will I make it?

Leadership Choices FrameWork

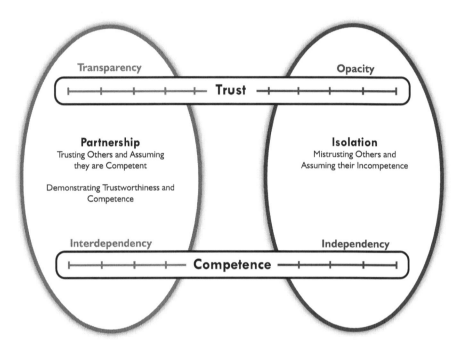

Key Points about Leadership Choices FrameWork

- In times of doubt, many people move towards mistrust and isolation.

- Moving towards partnership is a leadership choice in the midst of doubt.

- Increasing an awareness of the "hooks" that pull one towards isolation is necessary.

- Managing a team's level of trust is continual because partnership is more relational than conditional and "stuff" happens daily to everyone.

Key Questions

- What words, actions, and events have influenced me/us to move towards isolation in the past days/weeks/months?

- What words, actions and events have influenced me/us to move towards partnership in the past days/weeks/months?

- What patterns exist in responses to the previous two questions?

- What three things do I/we need less of to increase our partnership?

- What three things do I/we need more of to increase our partnership?

Chapter 2: Guiding Change

If you read and listen to the news, you know that public schools have been facing significant budgetary challenges. States are reducing school funding and sometimes delaying scheduled payments to school districts in order to get through an immediate financial shortfall. Consider the following scenario:

A large urban school district with an annual budget of $500 million is facing reduced state aid and must cut next year's budget by a minimum of $30 million. The superintendent and school board have to come up with a plan that targets where and how the cuts will be made. It might involve closing schools, consolidating and relocating others, reconfiguring busing, laying off teachers and administrators.

Before voting on the proposed plan, the school board holds several informational meetings for parents and interested residents. People are upset about the planned school closings and relocations. The affected parents don't want to move their children to a different school, and they don't want to be responsible for transporting them. Some are upset about a possible increase in class sizes. Many assume that less administration is an automatic "improvement in value" to the community.

"Change" Happens

In Chapter 1, I talked about how we respond when "stuff" happens—whether we reaffirm partnership or let ourselves slide toward doubt, mistrust, defensiveness, and isolation. The assumption is that stuff will indeed happen—on a daily basis. And it does, doesn't it? People will make mistakes, behave badly, get under our skin. We shouldn't be surprised when this happens, but we also shouldn't let ourselves become hardened to those around us and build up a protective wall of isolation and protectionism.

"Stuff" happening is a constant. It is change and it is natural. But although the inevitability of change would appear to be self-evident, we often behave as if it were not. We sometimes get bent out of shape when something changes, as if the way of the world were unbroken predictability and stasis.

In our defense, there is a good deal of predictability in the world. Indeed, the scientific enterprise is based on the notion of repeatability: observing the same results over and over again. We know, for example, when full solar and lunar eclipses have occurred in the past, and we know when they will happen in the future.

On the other hand, although we know when earthquakes and tornadoes have happened in the past, we can't predict with certainty when the next one will occur. We live simultaneously in a world of regular planetary and seasonal progression, and irregular daily variety—in a world of climate and a world of weather.

So we really shouldn't be surprised by change. And what's true "out there" is true internally as well. People change. I change. My wife and I have been married for more than 30 years. I'm not the same person now as the one she married (and she is grateful). She's not the same person that I married (although we both agree her need for change was less than mine). Our marriage today is not what it was 30+ years ago. It's not simply that we've aged. As life happens, we keep adapting, learning, changing—gratefully, gracefully (usually), and thankfully.

The great UCLA basketball coach John Wooden used to tell his players at the first practice, "At the end of the season, you'll either be a better player or a worse player than you are now." As human beings, changelessness is not an option.

Think back to a year ago. Are you a better or worse person and leader than you were one year ago? What would your colleagues say? What would your family and friends say?

The question, then, is not whether things and people will change. How we experience change determines whether our stories of change are "good" or "bad." The question, then, is how we respond to change when it occurs.

At least that's one question. Here's another one: How can a person design and manage change rather than simply react to it?

Putting the question this way doesn't alter the inevitability of change, but it suggests that there are strategies for guiding change. As you might expect by now, I think partnership is one of those strategies, and I use a FrameWork called Guiding Change to guide the partnership work when moving in a new direction.

Guiding Change FrameWork

Figure 4

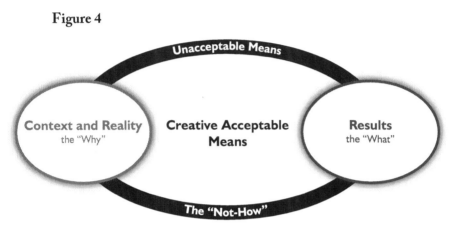

In the scenario I posed at the beginning of this chapter, a school board must cut its budget and has come up with a plan that generates community opposition. The facts are clear: There will be less money to work with next year. Changes must be made.

Using the language of the Guiding Change FrameWork, the "what" is reducing school district expenses by $30+ million while implementing key initiatives to improve learning and close the achievement gap. The "why" is a state legislative decision to delay funding by that amount. The why also includes all the realities the district must deal with: how many students it enrolls and where in the district they live, what its fixed assets are, what contractual obligations it has with staff, and so on. The question facing the board is "how" to achieve the necessary results.

Is There an End in Sight?

One approach to managing change can be called "end-determined." In our scenario, the superintendent and school board have come up with a plan to achieve a necessary result. They know what the end is. If they also determine exactly how that end will be reached, their only responsibility to their constituents is to inform them of the plan's details and implementation schedule. That could be done through the media and/or at a public meeting.

Figure 5

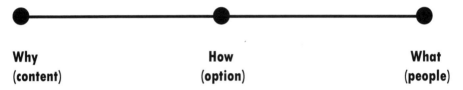

Why	How	What
(content)	**(option)**	**(people)**

End-determined decision making does not involve partnership; it means exercising delegated authority and control. It's a "Manage When I Must" moment. It happens in the zone of control, where variables are low and predictability is high. Such action may be right, respectful, and responsible under conditions of extreme urgency and risk. But if urgency and risk are not high, there may be costs to such an approach: mistrust, resistance, sabotage, and a withholding of creativity and ownership.

End-determined decisions are further compromised if the process is made to seem as though others' input is being sought, when actually that's just window dressing. Decision makers might seek "public input" but see it as a necessary evil—"due diligence"—rather than public engagement. The difference will always be answered by a simple question: Was the original design truly changed by public input?

An alternative approach is "end-in-view." Here, the what and why are the same as the previous example, but the how is more fluid and not predetermined. With an end-in-view, a leader or leadership team can make a conscious decision to engage in the zone of partnership, where variability and predictability are moderate. One way of doing so is by including others in the change process—not as a mere rubber stamp but as empowered participants with real ability to influence the outcome.

Figure 6

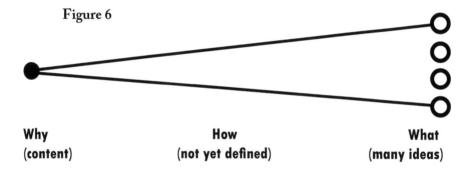

Why	How	What
(content)	**(not yet defined)**	**(many ideas)**

In the Guiding Change FrameWork scenario, the school board holds a series of meetings with teachers and parents. Let's imagine that at those meetings people come up with ideas the board has never considered, some that represent improvements on the existing plan. Is the board willing to alter its plan by incorporating those suggestions? If they are truly committed to partnership, the answer to that question must be "yes," or a clear reason must be offered for a "no."

Guiding the How

In creating a change scenario, I've streamlined the process considerably and left out plenty of messiness. If you've been in meetings where a group is trying to arrive at a decision or direction, you know that such efforts can be chaotic at times. Any time people try to do things as a group, some disorder will result, but there are ways to guide the process, to manage the "how."

One way is by carefully and firmly defining the question(s) at hand, what Glenda Eoyang calls the "container." A school board that asks, "How can we eliminate the achievement gaps among our various student populations?" is initiating a long-term discussion that will elicit all kinds of responses that may be too complex and wide-ranging to be actionable. That kind of big-picture question is important to ask, but it may not lead to productive group discussion at today's three-hour meeting. Narrowing the question(s) allows for constructive work that moves creative ideas from brainstorming to decision making to implementation. A possible alternative to the first question is, "What in-home parent engagement and teacher communication tools might best respond to the achievement gap data in reading at 2nd and 3rd grade?"

Another strategy for guiding group decision making is depicted in the FrameWork: specifying unacceptable means—the "not-how." Something could be unacceptable because it runs counter to a principle the organization is committed to. The not-how also includes actions that violate legal or contractual obligations. Unacceptable means are a good way of establishing parameters or boundaries which, in fact, enhance creativity and innovation, not stifle it. The sense of boundaries clarifies the scope and assists in creating an environment of innovation. Means should not be considered unacceptable, however, simply because, "We've never done it that way" or, "So-and-so doesn't like _____."

Group decision making can also be facilitated by distinguishing between divergent and convergent thinking. This is something Sam Kaner emphasizes.

Divergent thinking, says Kaner, might involve generating a list of ideas, whereas convergent thinking could involve sorting those ideas into categories. Divergent thinking stresses seeking diverse points of view; convergent thinking emphasizes coming to agreement. Exercising divergent thinking means resisting the itch for closure that I talked about in the last chapter.

We need to remember that there is a time to diverge and a time to converge. Effective group decision making means knowing the time and the purpose, which means managing the how.

Committing to Partnership

As I emphasized in the last chapter, partnership requires awareness, intention, and choice. If an individual or group says that the end is in view but undetermined and on the basis of that declared stance then solicits suggestions and critiques, those ideas must be taken seriously. More than that, decision makers must be willing to change their minds and their plans based on someone else's input or feedback. In short, don't ask for something unless you're prepared to use it.

In some situations, using the Guiding Change FrameWork means literally leaving the room. If a leader has defined a particular result, described the current context and reality, and specified the unacceptable means of achieving the desired result, the best strategy might be to leave. Leaving is a sign of trust in others' competence. It's a gesture that says, "We've set the conditions for you to do good work. Now go to it."

Operating in partnership is not without risk. For a choice maker, one risk is appearing indecisive. If the school board in our scenario goes on record with a plan for strategic change, invites public comment, and then changes the original plan, how will people respond? Some might be happy, but others will be critical:

"They're wishy-washy."

"We elected them to make decisions, not cater to special interest groups."

Operating in partnership means not only managing the change process but also managing one's own identity and image. I'll have more to say about how that works in the next chapter, but for now it can be said that image is important, and a leader—whether an individual or a group—should not appear to be indecisive. But partnership says that one can be decisive and flexible, visionary and accepting, transformational and collegial.

I should say one thing about authority here as well. In the introduction to this book, I emphasized that hierarchy, while beset with limitations, is not inherently bad. Indeed, hierarchy is natural and good in many human organizations, and attempts to eliminate it are unnatural and unproductive. The same is true of authority. In the scenario I described in this chapter, the superintendent and the school board have authority that was conferred by the election and appointment process. That delegated authority is natural and good. Citizens elect school boards, and school boards choose superintendents. A school board is an example of representative government. People should and do expect an elected board to represent their interests, and exercising the authority implicit in the electoral process is not an abuse of power.

If an individual or group that has achieved his, her, or their leadership position by legitimate means announces that an irrevocable decision has been made, that's not an abuse of authority. But having made a decision to involve others in the process, having invited their suggestions and contributions, and then reverting to a command-control mode of operating is disingenuous. Worse, such behavior is destructive—of morale, of trust, of organizational culture.

In the life of any organization, there will be decisions that must be made unilaterally. Sometimes it will be impractical to educate others sufficiently about the details of a problem to bring them in on the decision. Sometimes time constraints will preclude a larger discussion. Sometimes a particular individual or group will have obvious expertise that should be leveraged. Sometimes the buck simply has to stop here. As previously mentioned this is called, "Manage When I Must."

But whereas any leader will sometimes have to be "the choice maker," in any organization the opportunities for partnership will be abundant. Effective leaders recognize those opportunities and take advantage of them. In so doing, they help create a culture of partnership that characterizes the entire organization.

The operating principle that I preach to the people I work with is "Partner when WE Should & Manage when I Must." But you have to be consistent. Sparky Anderson, the former baseball manager, used to tell his players, "If you decide to slide, S-L-I-D-E." An indecisive base runner risks injury and increases the chances of being thrown out.

In a similar vein, I would say, "If you decide to partner, P-A-R-T-N-E-R." Remember that partnership is a choice and capacity of everyone in the organization. And if you need to manage, M-A-N-A-G-E with fairness, consistency, and efficiency. An indecisive or inconsistent manager risks injuring organizational culture, reducing performance and increasing the odds of being mistrusted and becoming isolated. Managing in such a simple and direct way builds trust for partnership. It does not work the other way—ever.

Committing to partnership means that you must be willing to walk away, let go of the pilot's wheel, return to the drawing board, defer to a better idea, change your mind. Committing to partnership means that you don't ask for input unless you really want it and unless that input has the potential to trump your own.

And here's the clincher: Being committed to partnership means that if the deliberative process produces a course of action that's clearly superior to the one you came up with, you have to support and champion the new choices as much as you would one of your own. In short, you must be willing to own something that you didn't think of.

The dynamics of partnership are not unlike those of being an adoptive parent. I know a couple who tried for several years to have a child, without success. They decided to adopt, and Tony, a winsome Korean baby, became part of their family. Two years later, Barb got pregnant and Micah joined brother Tony. Now Barb and Jim have a family of four. Their two sons look very different, but there is no difference in how their parents treat them, or refer to them, or present them to the world. One son is bone of their bone and flesh of their flesh. One came from different birth parents. Both are equally loved, equally disciplined, equally praised, equally bragged about.

Partnership is not about controlling everything, but is a matter of adapting to life in the context of organizational or personal purpose, mission, and vision. It may not be convenient or easy, and choosing it means not taking the path of least resistance.

Change as Opportunity

I began this chapter by observing that change is inevitable and I've been discussing how the Guiding Change FrameWork illustrates a way to manage change effectively. I want to conclude with a few remarks about how our attitude toward change affects our capacity to respond to it creatively.

I have a friend who lives in Minnesota and whose 86-year-old father, Ed, lives in Arizona. Ed's wife died several years ago, and shortly after that he moved into an assisted living facility in Tucson, where his other daughter lives. It was a big adjustment for him to be alone after a 60-year marriage, and it was an adjustment to live in an institution instead of his own home. He managed to make the transition pretty well, though, and now he likes where he lives.

The problem is that at the private facility where Ed lives, residents pay the full cost. It receives no Medicaid funds or other government support. Ed has been living off the proceeds of selling their house, and he'll run out of money within six months.

Fortunately, Ed is a veteran and the VFW is building a brand-new facility in Tucson. It's a state-of-the-art residence that will offer both assisted-living and skilled-care single rooms. Living there won't cost Ed anything, which means the pension he receives can be put toward other expenses. It sounds like a no-lose proposition.

But Ed doesn't want to move. He likes it where he is. He's made some friends there; he knows the staff and the routine; he's comfortable. His daughters, one in Tucson and one in St. Paul, see the VFW facility as an opportunity. Ed sees it as a threat.

There's no getting around it: change is hard. Human beings are creatures of habit, and we don't like being jarred out of our routines.

But change can be productive and renewing. At the microscopic level, our bodies must continuously replace cells in order for us to survive. At the macroscopic level, natural phenomena, like the water cycle, ensure the future of life on earth. In Walden, Henry David Thoreau wrote, "There is a constant influx of novelty into the world, and yet we tolerate incredible dullness." There is no need to tolerate dullness, and there is no reason to be afraid of novelty.

Change happens. What can we do to embrace change, to manage it rather than let it manage us? I'm convinced that partnership is one answer to that question.

In the end, what matters most is not the final decision Ed, makes but the partnership between Ed and his daughters in answering an end-of-life question. How many questions in your personal and professional life require greater partnership and less command and control?

Guiding Change FrameWork

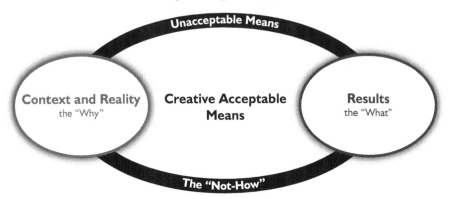

Key Points about Guiding Change FrameWork

- Use the FrameWork to "Partner When WE Should" without staying in the room.

- Maximize the level of detail in the Why/Reality and What/Results columns.

- Minimize the number of points in the Not How/Unacceptable Means column.

- Treat the Guiding Change document as something not set in stone, but a dynamic document reflecting the best and most recent knowledge and understanding among those in partnership.

Guiding Change Document: Key Steps and Questions

1. Define the Focus Issue or Question (this is the Title) Start by creating a relevant and manageable focus question. This should be a higher-order question, one that cannot be answered with a yes or no. The question must be narrow enough to focus a group's efforts productively, but inclusive enough to allow for creativity and innovation. For the Public School example, a Focus Question might be: *"How best can the district operate with a budget of $ xxxxx and successfully implement its strategic plans in the next year?"*

2. Define the current reality, the "why." Name the key assumptions operating today. Detail the relevant and compelling data. Review organizational policies and resources, and external trends and influences. Take advantage of demographic and market research. Describe the in-place barriers and blocks which need to be taken into consideration.

3. Describe the desired results, the "what." Define the measurable results as well as the organizational, cultural and relational conditions that go beyond the numbers.

4. Identify the unacceptable means, the "not-hows"—things the organization is not willing to do, based on philosophical, legal, contractual, and ethical commitments. Describe the parameters of what is not acceptable, especially if known tensions exist regarding some ideas and proposals.

Chapter 3:
Seeing Authority and Power

Ken has just been hired as Director of Human Resources at New Solutions Inc. Only four days into the job, he's told that a decision has been made to fire a long-time employee. As HR Director, Ken has to be the hatchet man.

Ken is in a quandary. He doesn't know the person who's being terminated, doesn't know the history of her involvement in the company, doesn't know how this firing will reverberate throughout the organization. And what's most unsettling is that Ken doesn't know how this first significant act as HR Director will affect his reputation and working relationships with his new colleagues.

Authority as Capital

Making a decision that affects others means exercising authority. As I noted in the previous chapter, authority—if rightfully practiced—is natural and good. Acting authoritatively is a hallmark of effective leadership, and deferring to legitimate authority is essential for the productive operation of groups and organizations.

To understand the dynamics of authority, it's necessary to recognize that there are three kinds; competency, organizational, and cultural authority. It's also helpful to think of authority as dynamic rather than static. Like other forms of capital, as one's authority is expended it needs to be replenished. If I spend down my capital in a particular area, I may need to build it back up again before using it in the future.

Using authority is a way of exercising power, and strategically exercising power means being able to size up a situation and determine what type of authority is called for. "Partner When WE Should **&** Manage When I Must" means being fully aware of your authority in three differing yet complementary dimensions and being aware of how your exercise of power is experienced by others.

To help people do that, I use the Authority and Power FrameWork as a reflection and action tool.

Figure 7 Authority and Power FrameWork

Cultural
Authority and Capital
(relationships and story)

Competency
Authority and Capital
(knowledge and experience)

Organizational
Authority and Capital
(title and position)

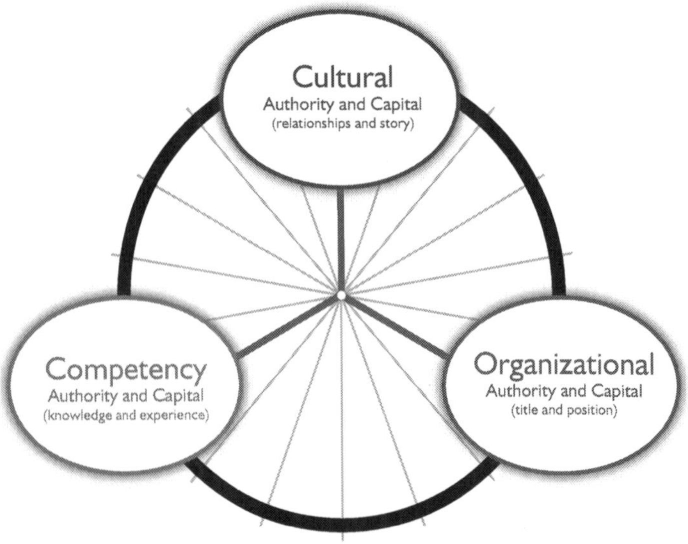

1. Competency authority and capital is what you develop by acting effectively. When you prove you are competent by meeting a challenge successfully, you build up capital. Competency can also be developed and demonstrated through education. Receiving specialized training and the degrees and certificates that go along with it shows competence, as does documented achievement on the job. Your résumé is a snapshot of your competency authority. Other forms of competency authority are acquired through experience, hobbies, and interests. When I work with groups, I often ask, "What competency do you have that's unique to this group?" A wide array of competency authority emerges, from arts to music to athletics to service.

2. Organizational authority and capital is what's conferred upon you by an employer. It's embodied in titles and job descriptions. We assume that a director will have more authority than an assistant director, and that both will defer to a vice president. A flowchart is a snapshot of organizational authority.

3. Cultural authority and capital is what's achieved by learning the ins and outs of a particular organization or group. This kind of authority can be institutional. As you learn about who reports to whom, about the history of interactions within and among groups, about the organization's reputation and story, you build up cultural capital. Cultural authority can also be relational. As you get to know personalities, rivalries, coalitions, grudges, friendships, which last names are important, etc.—and as people get to know you as a person—you accrue cultural capital. Cultural authority is complex and doesn't lend itself to a snapshot.

Taking Stock of Authority

In our scenario, Ken would benefit by assessing his situation in light of the three forms of authority.

As a new hire, Ken's competency authority exists mostly on paper. He has an MBA, and he served as HR Director for his previous employer. The people who hired him at New Solutions know about his work history, and they've read the glowing letters of recommendation that accompanied his application for his current position. But most of Ken's colleagues aren't privy to that information. They judge each other's competence by what people do, and Ken hasn't had a chance to do anything yet.

As HR Director, Ken has quite a bit of organizational authority, which is implicit in his job title. That authority came with the job, and Ken would lose it only if he lost his position.

Because he's only been on the job for a few days, Ken has very little cultural authority. In preparing for his interview, he did as much research as he could about New Solutions. But that told him only what any outsider could learn. He doesn't yet have any insider knowledge. Let's take a closer look at the three authority types and see if there's a way to resolve Ken's situation.

Competency Authority

In most organizations, the greater the competency the greater the compensation. Most of us want our efforts to be recognized and our success to be rewarded. Cronyism and nepotism are suspect because they sometimes reward people who haven't earned it.

The idea that authority and power should be based on competency is commonsensical and is evident in many areas of life. Parents, for example, mete out decision-making authority to children based on their demonstrated competence. Let's say your 13-year-old daughter wants to go to a party at the house of someone you don't know. Should you let her? That depends on all kinds of things, but one important consideration is her track record. If you're comfortable with her friends that you do know, if she consistently abides by curfews, if she has voluntarily removed herself from unhealthy situations in the past, then you're likely to trust her judgment in this instance.

The dynamics of competency authority could be illustrated in a Biblical story, often called the Parable of the Talents. A man was about to set off on a journey. Before leaving, he called for three of his servants. As recounted in the book of Matthew, "To one he gave five talents, to another, two, and to another, one, each according to his own ability."

The boss, in other words, made a judgment about his employees based on his assessment of their competency. When he returned, he found that the first servant had traded his five talents (a sizeable sum of money) and gained five more. Similarly, the servant with two talents earned two more. These employees were each praised: "Well done, good and faithful servant. You were faithful with a few things; I will put you in charge of many things."

The third servant, on the other hand, earned only his employer's wrath. Fearing the prospect of losing his one talent in the marketplace, he hid it in the ground. When the master returned and got the one talent back, he was furious and ordered that the hapless servant be "cast into outer darkness."

The Parable of the Talents illustrates that competency authority is a form of capital. The servants who were willing to invest their talents not only gained financially, they also validated the trust their employer put in them and earned a promotion. Investment always carries an element of risk. But the message of the story seems to be that risking failure is better than not risking at all.

Of course, most employers are not as harsh as the one in the parable. If you've achieved a certain level of competency and are then content to rest on your laurels, you're not likely to be cast into outer darkness. But you're also unlikely to advance in a system that rewards people based on achievement.

Competency authority is hard to get and extremely hard to lose. Once you've achieved certain abilities, credentials, and experience, no one can take them away from you. In the workplace, however, one must be aware that competency is both a fact and a judgment. I can be extremely competent, but if others with higher organizational authority don't see, believe, or value it, I might not hold the same authority at work that I hold outside the workplace.

Organizational Authority

Organizational authority, as the term suggests, applies to how authority is earned and delegated in most organizations. But just as we saw with competency authority, the getting and spending of organizational authority happens in all kinds of groups. In a family, for instance, we take for granted the validity of parental authority. Rare is the beleaguered mother who—challenged by a persistent child's "Why?"—has not at some point resorted to the response, "Because I'm your mother."

Implicit in that statement is the idea that some authority comes with the job and the title. Similar expectations apply in other realms. The orchestra members who show up for the first rehearsal of the season don't expect to decide how the rehearsal will be conducted. That's the conductor's job. Why? Because she's the conductor.

In large organizations, the lines of authority can be complex, and the question "Who do you report to?" achieves heightened significance. Adding to the complexity that employees in such organizations experience is the fact that organizational authority isn't always consistent with competency. In a given circumstance, your boss might not know more than you do.

The conflict between competency and organizational authority also surfaces in families. In the previous chapter, I gave the example of Ed, his two adult daughters, and the question of where he should live. How should the daughters respond if it's no longer the case that father knows best? In many families, this conflict comes to a head with driving. When do you take away the car keys? And who is the best person to do that?

On the job, conflicts can develop even when competency is not in question. For example, how do the two parties behave when a supervisor is considerably younger than a supervisee? Even if the supervisor's competency is well-established and accepted, a significant age differential can make things awkward. That's because we assume that organizational authority will reflect seniority. Usually it does, but what happens when it doesn't?

The wise leader does not use organizational authority reflexively or cavalierly. "Because I'm the boss" probably shouldn't be one's first line of defense or offense. On the other side, the wise subordinate does not challenge organizational authority willy-nilly. In a well-functioning organization, people recognize the legitimacy of hierarchy and the authority that goes along with it.

Organizational authority is easy to get and hard to lose. It comes with a job title, and it disappears only in the case of a demotion or dismissal. Although organizational authority is always there, it's usually the least effective kind of authority.

Another important thing about organizational authority is that it isn't static. As Barry Oshry points out, all of us function as Tops, Middles, and Bottoms, depending on the circumstances. Organizational authority is both structural and situational. You're a Top, for example, if you've been given responsibility for heading up a particular project. But if that project depends on action from those higher up, you become a Middle or a Bottom. The so-called "middle manager" can be one of the most stressful positions in an organization, beset as it often is by competing priorities and pressures from both above and below, often without direct control or influence of the human and financial resources necessary to get something done.

Organizational authority is fluid in another sense as well in that one can choose to sharpen or soften its lines. A common way to do this is with names and titles. Let's say you're a middle manager who's meeting with the company president, Joan Greenberg. In the course of conversation, you address her as Ms. Greenberg. She replies, "Please call me Joan."

Giving a subordinate permission to call you by your first name is a way of softening the lines of organizational authority. In other instances, one might choose to sharpen a line. Some pastors expect to be addressed by their title and no first names, even in casual conversation. It's rare to address a bishop or senator by first name, except in very personal and private situations.

Cultural Authority

What's the lay of the land? We use that metaphor to describe the challenge of encountering a new situation and figuring out what's what. If it's your first day in a new job, a new school, a new class, a new church, a new neighborhood, what do you want to know? If you're like me, you want an answer to the question, "How do things work around here and who are the 'who's' who matter?"

A friend, Tom, told me about what happened when he was hired as a teacher at a small college. He showed up early for the first faculty meeting and took a seat by himself. A woman who was on the search committee that had interviewed him came into the room, saw Tom sitting alone, and plunked herself down next to him. From that point until the meeting started, she gave Tom a capsule summary of each person who entered the room. "That's Greg Collins. He's Chair of the Arts, Communication, and Philosophy Division. That's Jill Foster. She's Chair of Science, Behavior, and Math. She and Greg don't get along. That's Barb Berman. She's Jill's support person, not faculty or administration, but she pretty much runs things around here."

And so on and so on. "It was a short course in organizational and human dynamics," said Tom. "Of course, I only got one person's view of things. But it helped me hit the ground running."

Cultural anthropologists know that the key to successful field work is finding the best informants. As James Spradley and David McCurdy observe in their book The Cultural Experience, "a good informant is one who knows the culture well." In an organization, such a person tends to be a hub of information, someone whose experience ranges across groups and departmental lines.

Of course, no single person will be able to provide a complete view of the culture he or she is part of. To get the whole picture you have to talk with more than one individual. And talking with insiders is only part of what's involved in learning a new culture. Much can be absorbed simply by observing people as they go about their work.

What's important about any of the ways one gains cultural knowledge is that they can't be accomplished from sitting in the office. In the words of author John le Carré, "A desk is a dangerous place from which to view the world." To get the lay of the land, you have to get out and experience it. In their book In Search of Excellence, Tom Peters and Robert Waterman call this "management by wandering around" or MBWA. As the term "wandering" implies, this form of management isn't systematic. It's informal rather than formal, personal rather than institutional.

MBWA works best when you exude a relaxed attitude, watch and listen without judgment, and project the image of a collaborator rather than an inspector. Besides helping one determine the lay of the land, MBWA helps build collegiality and trust, makes managers more approachable, and provides opportunities to reinforce cultural values.

MBWA is especially important in an age of ever-increasing reliance on electronic communication. No one can afford to ignore the email inbox, but letting yourself be tyrannized by email, text messages, and tweets will result in a serious curtailment of cultural authority.

Cultural authority is hard to get and very easy to lose. It's the most powerful and yet the most tenuous authority to manage. To maintain your store of cultural authority, you have to keep paying attention to it, and you can't always say or do the culturally-combative thing, even if you think it is needed. Pushing too hard against organizational culture can risk a "fund" of hard-earned cultural authority.

A key note here is that some organizations operate with institutional cultural authority, which one either has or doesn't have. Institutional cultural authority provides clarity regarding authority—but also confusion and conflict when it's misused. The three institutions where I've seen this most clearly are the church (priests), medicine (physicians), and higher education (tenured faculty). In each setting, those with institutional cultural authority operate with a "fifth ace in the sleeve" compared to others, and it is culturally important to the organization that others know the difference. Operating in these systems require this awareness, acknowledgement, and acceptance. It is the culture and it is the institution. In these types of organizational cultures, there are unspoken authority differences that heavily influence other relationships; there are perceived risks to challenging a physician, professor, or pastor after they have stated their position or want.

When using the Power and Authority FrameWork, the issue of political capital usually emerges in a learning conversation. Political capital is a combination of the three authorities in the FrameWork but is largely made up of cultural authority. Politics is the art of acquiring, organizing, and using the resources of an organization, system, or community to advance one's philosophy, beliefs, goals, and agenda. This skill requires a high level of cultural knowledge, experience, and capital. For many, alliances are required to accumulate cultural authority, access the competency and organizational authority needed for legitimacy, and access to the information needed to use and build political capital.

Authority in Action

Let's get back to Ken, our HR Director. As you'll recall, he was faced with the difficult assignment of informing a long-time employee that she was being terminated when he himself had been on the job only a few days. Ken started by taking inventory of his own authority. He concluded that his strong suit was organizational authority, embodied in his job title. His competency authority was largely unknown by everyone in the company except for the people who hired him. His cultural authority was nonexistent and thus so was his political capital.

Ken knew that his organizational authority was sufficient for him to carry out the directive from his superiors. But he also sensed that firing a long-time employee would result in a significant drain of organizational capital and that he would be wise not to rely solely on this resource.

Recognizing that he had no cultural authority at New Solutions, Ken decided it would be a good idea to talk with other people in the company to learn more about how the employee whom upper management had deemed "troublesome" was perceived by her colleagues. Dismissing this individual would be a "cultural" event at the company, and he knew he would not survive his first year of employment.

Ken discovered that the employee was well-respected by both peers and subordinates. Although some found her occasionally abrasive, she was consistently described as knowledgeable, competent, and fair.

Based on what he learned from these conversations, Ken concluded that if he terminated the employee, it would take a long time to build trust and respect at New Solutions and restore his depleted organizational capital. He also feared that too much grumbling in the ranks might make him expendable.

Ken brought his concerns to upper management and explained the costs of the action they were asking him to make. He suggested an alternative: As HR Director, he would work closely with the employee to collaborate on a plan that would involve monitoring, regular reporting, and professional development. He asked his superior to set their sights further out than immediate termination. Recognizing the predicament, they agreed. In the end, the employee was retained and even promoted. In this case, developing a human resource was a more effective approach than discipline.

Amplifying and Softening Authority

As I've observed, authority is not static. We can take deliberate steps to soften, sharpen, broaden, or narrow authority and power depending on the demands of a particular situation. Those steps can be both verbal and nonverbal. Most of what I have to say in this section is addressed to those in a position of power: to Tops in relation to Middles and Bottoms, or Middles in relation to Bottoms. I'm also interested in those situations where authority and power are contested.

One component of competency authority is educational achievement. I have a friend who has a Ph.D. and spent most of her life in an academic setting. In her late 40's she decided to leave the university where she was working and pursue a career as a writer and editor. She had published extensively in scholarly journals and edited one for several years. The jobs she would be applying for, however, were not in the academic setting. She didn't want to come across to prospective employers as an egghead, but her relevant experience was almost all academic. To enhance her image in a new field, she decided not to list all her publications and conference presentations on her résumé, electing to include only those whose titles suggested the widest possible audience and applicability. Furthermore, on some versions of her résumé she left out her Ph.D.

My friend was trying to broaden what she feared would be a narrow perception of her competency authority by de-emphasizing some things. In other situations a person might choose to play up competency. If you've left a message at your cardiologist's office and get a response, the physician is likely to say, "This is Dr. Fisher returning your call." Using a professional title reinforces both competency and organizational authority, and you'll probably feel more confident in a doctor's expertise if she self-identifies that way than if she says, "Hi, this is Nancy Fisher."

If you show up for an appointment with Dr. Fisher, you no doubt expect her to be wearing a white lab coat, whereas the LPN who checks your pulse might be dressed in something different. Attire is a powerful nonverbal way of demonstrating authority. In some kitchens, only the head chef wears a toque. The priest with a collar signals a set-apart status reinforcing spiritual authority, just as the judge in a robe is reinforcing legal authority.

Earlier in my career I worked for a large corporation as an engineer. When visiting a company plant in a rural area for the first time, I packed a suit. When I arrived, I checked into the hotel, put my suit on, and drove to the plant. When I stopped at the front desk, the receptionist asked if I had blue jeans with me. I said "no" and wondered what she meant by that question.

Just then the plant manager walked in, took one look at me, and pointed out the door. "Young man," he said sternly, "you may not come into our plant dressed like some big shot from the cities. Go to K-mart, get some blue jeans and clothes you can get dirty in, and come back in an hour."

The plant manager did me a huge cultural favor by informing me of local norms of which I was ignorant. The receptionist later laughed with me at how dumbfounded I had looked. When I returned to my office the next week, my boss had a chuckle at my expense. He told me to wear a new suit—as a lesson. In the end, I realized everyone was trying to help me be successful.

I mentioned clergy and judges in relation to attire. They're also examples of another dimension of nonverbal authority: physical position. The judge sits at a "bench," which is elevated. In some churches, the pulpit is raised above the level of the platform. In discussing what they call "orientational metaphors,"

George Lakoff and Mark Johnson note that high status is up and low status is down (She's at the peak of her career. He's at the bottom of the heap.). Where you position yourself, then, carries a message.

The rooms in most office buildings don't have stages, so literally elevating yourself at a staff meeting usually isn't an option. But if everyone else is sitting and you're standing, your posture is an implicit claim of authority. At an oblong conference table, do you sit at the head of the table, in the middle, or at 10 or 2 relative to the head position? In a room with a lectern, do you stand behind it? Your decision in those situations should be deliberate and strategic, depending on your relative need for power and authority in a particular instance.

Another example of the messages implicit in physical location is offices and desks. At a growing social networking company headquartered in New York City, everyone—including the executives—works at tables in an unpartitioned room. If people need a more private setting for a conversation, they can use a conference room, but in so doing they're always in neutral space, never on one person's turf. There is no such thing as a private office.

If you do have a private office with a desk, is there also a table with two or more chairs? If so, what is signaled by moving from behind your desk and taking a seat with your conversational partner(s) at the table?

I started this section with examples of verbal ways to play up or play down one's authority, then moved to several nonverbal examples. Let me conclude the section with some more thoughts about how our words affect the way we're perceived.

How We Say What We Say Makes A Difference

The sociolinguist Deborah Tannen has written extensively about the function of language in a variety of human relationships, both personal and work-related. She distinguishes between what she calls "report talk" and "rapport talk." The purpose of report talk is to inform, to negotiate, to argue. Most meetings are dominated by report talk. The purpose of rapport talk, on the other hand, is to establish connections and explore relationships. Report talk consists mostly of statements. Rapport talk includes more questions.

In report talk, Tannen says, people tend to use language to assert power over others. In rapport talk, they use language to reinforce partnership with others. And because of the dynamics of report talk, statements often trump questions in that setting, as is illustrated in a situation that occurred at a conference Tannen attended. A speaker gave a talk, which was followed by a Q&A session. An audience member (I'll call her Ann) said, "It sounds like you're saying X. Have you ever considered Y?" The speaker responded by reasserting his commitment to X. Later, another audience member (I'll call him Ben) said, "I want to come back to something that was said earlier. You're saying X, but it's clear to me that Y is a superior position." A lively debate ensued, involving the speaker and several other audience members, during which people who referred to position Y attributed it to Ben, even though it was Ann who first expressed it. Because Ann cast her remark as a question rather than a statement, Tannen observes, it had less impact in a forum dominated by report talk.

So which is better, statements or questions? The answer, of course, is that it depends on what your purpose is. If you're trying to advance a discussion and are not concerned about asserting power, then questions may serve well. But if you want to reinforce your authority, asking questions might be less effective.

The point in all these examples, verbal and nonverbal, is that our words and actions are inevitably bound up with issues of authority and power. Thinking about the three kinds of power, how they are accumulated and spent, is a vital component of effective leadership and a key to productive working relationships.

Authority and Partnership

In the introduction to this book, I used the example of a boss's sudden appearance at an informal meeting in the staff lounge to illustrate the sometimes dampening effect that authority can have on people's work. In the presence of authority, some people tend to clam up or otherwise alter their normal way of behaving and relating. I also noted that those in positions of authority are usually dismayed at such responses.

Effectively exercising authority and the power that goes with it is facilitated by practicing partnership. Based on the discussion in this chapter, we're now in a position to reflect further on how principles of partnership affect the acquisition and disposition of authority.

As I've previously observed, partnership recognizes differences in authority and power. Partnership does not equal egalitarianism. But partnership does involve give and take, and in a given instance it may mean that someone with greater authority defers to someone with less—if doing so serves the greater good.

The act of deferring—of temporarily ceding one's authority—could be perceived as portraying weakness. But I think it's just as likely to be seen as a strength, and it's also likely to counter the negative effect a leader's presence sometimes has on subordinates. If the boss in our staff lounge meeting scenario had a history of partnership, her sudden appearance there probably wouldn't have caused a ripple. Indeed, she might have been asked to join in.

Partnership in Hollywood

Let me close this chapter by referring to a popular movie that powerfully illustrates the dynamics of authority and partnership.

Hoosiers is set in the fictional rural town of Hickory, Indiana, a hotbed of basketball fever. Norman Dale arrives there to be a high school teacher and basketball coach. Jimmy Chitwood, the best player from the previous year, has announced that he does not intend to play this year. Dale's colleague, Myra Fleener, tells him not to try and get Chitwood to change his mind. She thinks Jimmy needs to concentrate on his studies and earn an academic scholarship in order to attend college.

The coach starts off as suspect in the eyes of many townspeople when they learn that he's been in the Navy recently and hasn't coached for 10 years. He further alienates the community by dismissing a key player who violates his strict disciplinary rules and by insisting on a deliberative style of play that doesn't produce immediate results.

Analyzing Norman Dale's situation in light of the Authority and Power FrameWork, it's evident that his competency authority is shaky. His immediate job experience doesn't seem relevant for his current position, and starting the season by losing doesn't help matters. Dale's organizational authority is established: He was hired as the basketball coach, and his word holds—at least for now. As a newcomer to the town and the school, he starts with no cultural authority and thus neither cultural or political capital.

In an early scene, Dale is invited to a meeting with most of the town's men that proves to be an important source of cultural knowledge. He learns that everyone has an opinion about the basketball team, including what kind of defense they should play, and that the unanimous conviction is that success hinges on getting Jimmy Chitwood to play. He also gets hints that his future as a coach lies in the townspeople's hands.

After the team loses several games and Dale has made no effort to woo Chitwood, a town meeting is called to vote on whether he should be fired as basketball coach. Dale gives a short speech in which he refuses to apologize, asserts his confidence and pride in the team, and says that he's done what he was hired to do: teach basketball. The vote goes against him, but just after the result is declared, Jimmy Chitwood shows up and announces that he's decided to join the team—but only if the coach is allowed to stay. Another vote is called for, and this time it goes in Dale's favor.

With Chitwood in the fold, the team embarks on a winning streak. Dale diffuses his own authority by asking a player's father (the town drunk but a knowledgeable basketball fan) to be an assistant coach, insisting that the man clean up his act. Dale even deliberately gets himself thrown out of a game in order to give the assistant a spot in the limelight.

This being Hollywood, the team makes it to the finals of the state tournament, where they're matched against a taller team from a much larger school. The game, as it must, comes down to one chance for the team from Hickory to break a tie and win.

During a time-out to set up the final play, Dale announces that because everyone will be expecting Jimmy Chitwood to take the last shot, they should set up the play for another player. Rather than breaking the huddle and going back on the floor, the team members hesitate, looking nervously at each other. "What's wrong?" Dale asks. No one wants to speak, but it's obvious that they don't agree with the coach's plan. Finally, Chitwood says, "I'll make the shot."

It's what might be called a partnership moment. Norman Dale is the coach. He could pull rank and order his players to carry out his instructions. But he's facing five adolescents who started the season as a collection of individuals and have become a team. He's seen them grow in ability and confidence. He recognizes that a level of collective wisdom has emerged that rivals his own. And so he cedes to the group. The players run back on the floor, and you know how it ends. This is Hollywood, after all.

Partnership isn't always natural and sometimes isn't easy. It doesn't guarantee success in any given venture, but practiced consistently, I'm convinced that it's the best way for individuals and organizations to grow and prosper.

Authority and Power

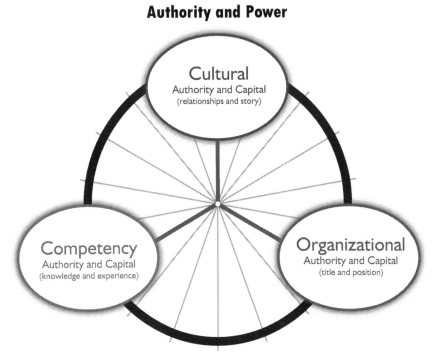

Key Points about Authority and Power FrameWork

- Always be aware of your level of capital in each of three authority arenas and your political capital.

- Assess what forms and combinations of authority and capital work most effectively in the culture of the group or organization.

- Play "chess" by maintaining a list of the anticipated future authority "plays" you and others need to make. Strategize accordingly. Choose delegation, alliances, and partnerships over direct use of cultural capital unless it is absolutely needed.

- Challenge the misapplication or ineffective use of authority by others. Do so courteously and tactfully, perhaps privately rather than publicly.

Key Steps and Questions

Assess your authority and capital in relation to the situation and those who will be affected by the decision. Map these assessments on the FrameWork. Ask yourself some key questions:

1. What combination of authority/capital is needed for the action you are about to take?

2. To what extent will this action use up a particular kind of authority?

3. To what extent do you need to build up capital before undertaking this action?

4. Will this action be best facilitated by sharpening or softening lines of authority and power differences?

5. How will this action affect the balance of power in the group or organization?

Chapter 4:
Managing Transitions

At Fairview Elementary School, the staff received a district mandate to implement a revised curriculum that emphasizes teaching literacy in all subjects. Although enthusiasm for the new program was high when the school year started, by November complaints were frequent and commitment seemed questionable. To address what she perceived as growing discontent, the principal called a staff meeting to discuss the literacy curriculum.

At the meeting, some teachers were vocal in their opposition to the new program, while some spoke passionately in favor of it. Others said the new approach needed more time to prove itself, and some seem surprised by all the fuss. Faced with a lack of agreement, the principal adjourned the meeting without coming to a conclusion about a course of action.

Who Do You Serve?

Human beings are social creatures. For most of us, the way we see ourselves has much to do with how we imagine others see us. Philosophers from

Plato on forward have observed that the moral character of a people is shaped by the groups that individuals form. Human history is an ongoing study in the dialectic between individualism and community.

In the U.S.A., we've always placed a strong emphasis on individual liberty and have resisted what we see as encroachments on our freedom. At the same time, most Americans recognize the importance of groups and are willing to give up some personal freedoms to sustain the existence of collectivities from which they draw nurture and support.

The first group one usually experiences is the family, where the growing child quickly learns that her freedom is constrained by the people she lives with. Most parents want their children to become something other than copies of themselves, want them to develop as unique individuals with their own gifts and potential. Yet most parents also impose limitations on individual expression and teach their children to respect and sometimes defer to others.

From the family, children move on to school, where, for most, their membership in a classroom results in further constraints on their own impulses. While in school, students might join teams, clubs, religious organizations, and other groups in which being a member means fitting oneself with others, negotiating a balance between mine and thine.

Eventually, almost everyone gets a job and, even for the self-employed, going to work means relating to some kind of organization and navigating multiple organizations, whether a mom-and-pop store or a multinational corporation. Most of us want a job that provides a measure of personal satisfaction and self-fulfillment, and we also aspire work that transcends our own personal interests and abilities. We enjoy being part of something bigger than ourselves.

The idea that one's job has both a personal and social dimension is central to a conception of work suggested by a term that for many might sound old-fashioned: calling. "In a calling", wrote Bellah, Madsen, et al. (authors of Habits of the Heart: Individualism and Commitment in American Life), "committing one's self to becoming a good carpenter, craftsman, doctor, scientist, or artist anchors the self within a community practicing carpentry, medicine, or art. It connects the self to those who teach, exemplify, and judge these skills. It ties us to still others whom they serve."

Looking at work as a calling means striving to balance individual and group goals. It means being willing to subordinate one's desire for self-fulfillment to organizational fulfillment. Integrating individualism and service to others is at the heart of partnership.

The Personal is Political

In Chapter 2, I talked about the inevitability of change and the importance of managing change rather than simply reacting to it. Here I want to explore the dynamics of change further and show how transitions in organizations involve an interplay between individual and group experience.

No healthy organization remains static, and because any organization experiences continual cycles of transition, the responsibilities of its employees also evolve. A nimble organization must be able to respond to a variety of influences: new legislation, shifting markets, new competitors, and technological advances. A nimble employee, in turn, must be willing and able to adapt to different responsibilities and a revised job description.

The responsibility for assessing the environment in which an organization does business is generally assumed to be with its leaders—the Tops. Much of what I had to say in the previous chapter about exercising authority and power was addressed to that group. Here I'll be talking mostly to Middles and Bottoms—the people charged with implementing transitions that originate at the top. The Middles and the Bottoms also carry a leadership responsibility to assess, see, imagine, innovate, plan, and implement constructive and positive change to achieve organizational goals and vision.

To help individuals and groups deal with the personal and professional change that always accompanies organizational change, I use the Transition and Development FrameWork.

Figure 8: Transition and Development FrameWork

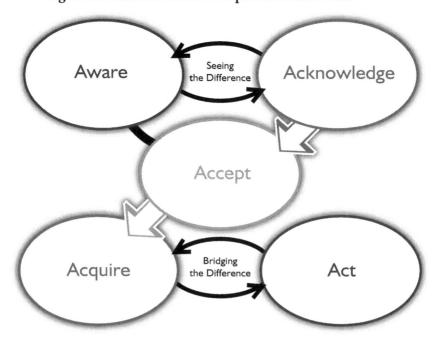

Awareness: Do You See What I See?

The first step in navigating an organizational transition is to become aware. Awareness means taking in information: seeing, hearing, understanding. For Tops, promoting awareness within the organization is facilitated by presenting information clearly, timely and concisely:

1. Here is the current reality, vision and conditions.

2. Here are the internal and external emerging influences operating on us.

3. Here are possible ways for us to respond.

4. Here is what it would take to make the change.

For Middles and Bottoms, becoming aware means listening carefully, reading thoughtfully, seeing politically, and questioning strategically. One's awareness at any given time is affected by one's frame of reference—the beliefs and values that function as a filter through which one processes new information.

At a purely sensory level, our brains must process sensory stimuli and translate them into sights and sounds and sensations that we can apprehend and make sense of. At a broader perceptual level, we depend on a cache of previous experiences to help us interpret and respond to new ones.

Peter Senge refers to one's frame of reference as "mental models" and sees those models as "so deeply held, we don't even realize they are there." My experience mirrors his assertion that "we don't have mental models, we *are* our mental models."

The anthropologist Clifford Geertz calls our collective fund of experience "culture", which he sees as what separates humans from other animals. Culture, in Geertz's view, is not something ornamental or optional. We don't acquire culture by going to the opera or visiting a museum. Instead, culture is the very means by which we make sense of things—a recipe for how to live in that part of the world we find ourselves in.

"Becoming human is becoming individual," writes Geertz, "and we become individual under the guidance of cultural patterns, historically created systems of meaning in terms of which we give form, order, point, and direction to our lives."

The historian of science Thomas Kuhn used the term paradigm to get at a similar truth. For Kuhn, a paradigm is the accumulated wisdom that enables what he calls "normal science." Scientists are able to do their work only because of paradigms: accepted ways of understanding reality and accepted methods of testing new theories.

A culture or paradigm could be seen as limiting, and most of us have felt a desire (especially as adolescents!) to break free from its shackles. But without the filtering and ordering effect of culture, argues Geertz, we would not even be human.

In the last chapter I talked about the importance of cultural capital—a sense of the lay of the land and the combination of authorities into political capital: acquiring and using resources. The fact that any organization has a particular culture—a way that members habitually understand, communicate, and behave—can lead Tops to short-circuit or overly simplify the information-dispensing stage of a transition because of an assumption that everyone shares a mutual understanding and processes information the same way. The truth, however, is that although a shared culture is necessary for perception and understanding, each of us processes our experiences differently.

Awareness, then, is both social and individual. And awareness has both an external and internal dimension. Externally, we must have eyes to see and ears to hear. We must seek out information. We must pay attention. We must look before we leap.

Internally, achieving awareness means recognizing our own and others' frames of reference, our mental models and paradigms. That recognition need not, in fact cannot, be constant. Indeed, the effectiveness of a model or filter depends on it usually operating beneath the level of conscious thought. But realizing that others might have different frames, their own ways of perceiving and interpreting experience, is an important part of being aware.

Acknowledgment: How Will This Affect Me?

Becoming aware of what a change will involve for me and others is the first step toward acting. The next stage involves acknowledging the implications of the change. How will things be different—for me, for my department or team, for the company—if we make this transition?

Clara is part of a writers group that formed after she took a class in memoir writing. When the class was over, several members decided to keep meeting on their own. They got together once a month to share their writing with each other. They took turns reading a selection to the group, who then responded with questions, observations, and suggestions.

After the group had been meeting for about a year, Gwen proposed a change. Instead of just listening to each other read, she suggested that people email their writing to the rest of the group a week or so before the meeting. "That way," she said, "we'll be better able to respond because we'll have had some time to think about what to say."

Most group members didn't see this as a very big change. They felt the way they'd been doing things had worked well, but they didn't have a problem with Gwen's proposal. The biggest difference, they thought, would involve getting something to group members in advance of the meeting.

For Clara, on the other hand, the new procedure represented a potentially significant change in group dynamics. "Because now we just hear each other's writing," she said, "we respond to the ideas, the style, the language, the images. I worry that if we see a text, we'll start correcting punctuation and grammar, and that's not what I'm looking for."

Gwen had done an adequate job of describing the proposed change. Other group members were aware of what it would involve. But whereas most of them thought any differences would be minor ones of process, Clara anticipated a major difference in experience. She was instrumental in helping the group anticipate how things would be quite different. Clara helped move the group from awareness to acknowledgment.

When a change is significant, it involves what Thomas Kuhn calls a paradigm shift. I call this a recognition of the differences that make a difference, given one's awareness of changes in the current reality and environment. In the history of science, one notable paradigm shift was the Copernican revolution, which meant changing from a conception of the solar system with Earth at the center to one where Earth and other planets orbit the sun.

Another major shift was from Newtonian to Einsteinian physics. At the end of the 19th century, the physicist Lord Kelvin declared, "There is nothing new to be discovered in physics now. All that remains is more and more precise measurement." Five years later, in 1905, Albert Einstein published his theory of special relativity, which challenged the understanding of force and motion that had ruled scientific thinking since the time of Newton. Einstein didn't see his theory as supplanting Newtonian physics but rather as accounting for things that the earlier understanding could not account for. Even as this chapter is being written, there is a new challenge to Einsteinian physics with the reported "faster than light" speed of neutrinos measured in Europe. Time will tell, yet the message is clear: Change is a constant—always.

Paradigm shifts don't happen overnight. Because they represent a major change, they're always challenged and contested. But eventually, if a new paradigm proves sound, it becomes standard operating procedure. For that to happen, the people involved must move from acknowledgement to acceptance.

Acceptance: Can I Live with This?

So, a transition has been proposed and explained. The people involved have been made aware of the new direction and have acknowledged its differences and implications. No real change will occur, though, without acceptance.

Accepting a change means not only understanding it but being willing to undertake it. This is the pivotal stage in transition and development, which is why it's at the center of the Transition and Development FrameWork.

Transition and Development FrameWork

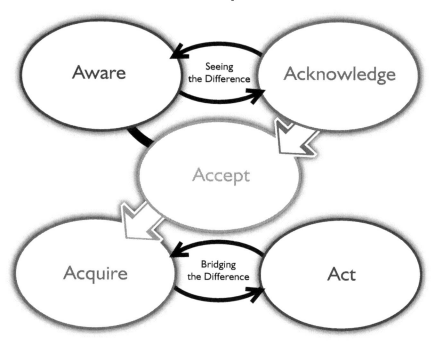

The graphic above has two lines leading from Accept. One moves to the next stage of Acquire; the other leads back to Aware. Some people, having achieved awareness and acknowledgement, will decide not to embrace a change. I call this line from Acceptance back to Awareness the "pathway of denial." Because one cannot or will not change, for whatever reason, one moves back to Awareness without the commitment to Accept to change and move forward.

One way to describe the shift in perspective that acceptance depends on is by invoking the idea of ownership. What does it mean to own something?

Acceptance and Ownership

Compare your feelings about something you've rented versus something you own. When you stay in a motel, you're renting a room for a set period at a set price. You're legally responsible to pay for the room and not damage its contents. After you've checked out, you have no continuing responsibilities. If the coffee maker in the room didn't work when you checked in and someone brought a different one, you don't have to worry about fixing the original.

Contrast that arrangement with owning the house you live in. As a property owner, you still have legal responsibilities. You must pay your mortgage every month and your property taxes twice a year. You must abide by local requirements regarding maintenance, enhancements, and so forth.

But whereas renting a room is almost completely defined by contractual matters, for most people, owning a home represents an emotional involvement as well. Because you know that others will judge you by what kind of home you own, you invest something of yourself in it. In a motel room, you live with whatever pictures are on the wall. In your house, you choose wall hangings carefully to reflect your tastes and experiences and what's important to you.

In deciding to own something, you make an investment and a commitment. And what's true for material objects is true for nonmaterial things as well. To "own" a problem is to assume responsibility for it. To own a decision is to commit yourself to seeing it through and living with the consequences.

One way of gauging whether someone has owned a decision is observing how that person reacts to adversity. If you truly own something, you will defend and protect it.

Owning something doesn't preclude modifying it. Many people who buy an existing house do some remodeling. But you don't easily abandon something you own, and you don't make changes lightly.

Acquire: What Do I Need?

Once you've decided to accept and "own" your change, you still might not be ready to act. Most significant changes require one to acquire something: resources, knowledge, expertise.

Responsibility at this stage of transition and development is shared. Tops are responsible for anticipating what their subordinates will need to accomplish a change. Middles and Bottoms are responsible for stating their needs clearly, respectfully, and firmly.

Perhaps the most common mistake I see organizations make at this stage is not allowing sufficient time. In chapter 1, I emphasized that playing the believing game, because it doesn't always come naturally, takes more time than the doubting game, which most of us play instinctively. Indeed, a commitment to partnership almost always means taking more time than would be involved in a command-control approach.

Acquire Requires Awareness - Acknowledgement - Acceptance

I am honored to do a lot of work with public school districts. One thing all educators are aware of these days is the achievement gap between white students and students of color, as well as the achievement gap between all students and the learning standards leading to college and career readiness.

When I talk to a group of teachers or administrators about this problem, I don't have to spend any time at the awareness stage. They know what the numbers, and who the students, are.

Acknowledging and accepting the achievement gap as "mine to own" is quite different. It means undergoing a paradigm shift—from an emphasis on teaching to an emphasis on learning, from a focus on curriculum to a focus on instruction, from seeing a class of students to seeing individual students. And ultimately that shift has to occur, not only among administrators and school board members, but among classroom teachers and students as well. In addition, acknowledgement requires ownership, at least of one's part, in the conditions, performance, and experience of self and others.

The achievement gap is not a local or regional phenomenon; it's a national one. It's come about for a variety of reasons, one of which is that what Paulo Friere and others have called the "factory model" of education is not well-suited to the cultural and economic diversity that has increasingly come to characterize most schools. Closing the achievement gap means changing the way of doing business in American schools, which is not something that's going to be done on the basis of a few staff meetings or new laws or one-time funding programs.

Let's assume that classroom teachers in a particular school have acknowledged the achievement gap and accepted their responsibilities, strengths, and weaknesses to address it. What do they need?

They need knowledge, skill, and cultural development for work and engagement they are not yet fully equipped to do. They need to learn how to identify their students' different learning styles and then how to develop teaching strategies that fit those styles. They need to accept that not everyone has to solve a problem the same way. They need to see the expectations gap, inspiration gap, and aspirations gap, as well as the consistent conditions of race, poverty, and wealth at the core of the achievement gap. They need to develop greater cultural awareness, to understand that different groups of people have different ways of seeing, understanding, arguing, justifying, interacting, and living. They need to broaden their understanding of their own role, from a dispenser of knowledge to a co-learner with their students.

Helping people acquire what they need is the responsibility of Tops and Middles. Far too many organizations don't provide adequate time for reflection and for development of their employees.

Acquire Can Take Many Forms

Many Japanese schools use an approach to planning called lesson study. With this method, a group of teachers collaborate to come up with a school-wide theme. They develop a broad research question and list skills, behaviors, and attitudes they want to cultivate. The group then works together to develop a specific lesson plan that addresses the theme and the shared goals. They create a template that shows how this lesson fits in the larger curriculum and how it connects to what's been taught previously and what comes next. The template also addresses how student learning will be assessed.

Next, the lesson is taught by one member of the group and observed by the other members. The purpose of the observation is not to critique the teacher's ability but to gauge students' learning. The group then discusses the lesson and their observations. Based on that discussion, the lesson is revised and taught by another group member. The process of observing, discussing, and revision is repeated.

Using this intensive approach, a group can work on two or three lessons a year, and the complete process can take several years to complete. How many U.S. schools would be willing to invest that much time in collaborative lesson planning? How many teachers in those schools would be willing to open their classroom door to colleagues?

For many professionals, the Transition and Development FrameWork has an important lesson: "one and done" training does not work for most people. Why? The first experience of new material, knowledge, or skill typically raises awareness. People say "that was interesting." They might feel informed, but until they acknowledge the difference that makes a difference and accept the challenge to change their professional practice, little of substance will be different.

If, on the other hand, one accepts to change, then encountering the same information can have a profound impact on the ability to listen, process, and learn. True acquisition requires acceptance.

Some Tops will announce a decision, expecting all to accept it and move to implementation based on the elegance of the message, or the authority of the presenter, or both. But it doesn't work that way for most people. Your announcement does not equal my instant processing, understanding, accepting, or acquiring capacity. Organizational life is a bit more complex and humane than that.

Action: So Now What Do I Do?

If the groundwork has been laid—if the relevant parties have moved through the steps of awareness, acknowledgement, acceptance, and acquiring—taking action should be the most straightforward part of the transition process. Most of the problems organizations have with transitions result from inadequate preparation and buy-in. Acting prematurely, acting without having the right people on board, acting without giving those people the time and resources to process a change before it occurs, acting without a clear plan—these are what lead to stalled projects that never reach their potential.

As I emphasized in Chapter 2, changes should be planned and organized, and should take place with what I call a Guiding Change document. This document represents information that a group of people share and principles they agree on. Once it's approved, it serves as a reference point for action. Six days or six weeks or six months down the road, if a question arises about how to act, referring back to the Guiding Change document will refresh people's minds about the reasons for the change, the steps to achieve it, and the desired outcomes.

Another valuable component of the action stage is what's been called a continuous improvement loop. As a change gets acted out, it's common for people to realize that there are some things they didn't anticipate. It might then be necessary to go back to the Acquire stage for more information. In the Framework, this likelihood is illustrated by arrows between the Acquire and Act stages.

In 1786 Robert Burns said, "The best-laid schemes of mice and men go oft awry." The fact is that despite our best efforts to prepare and anticipate, things rarely go exactly as planned. The FrameWork that anchors this chapter is called Transition and Development. In discussing the Acquire stage, I stressed the importance of giving people time to develop the knowledge and skills they will need to navigate a transition. That development occurs before acting. But development is not a "one-and-done" event. Instead, development should be seen as a continual part of the transition process.

The Transition and Development FrameWork in Action

It's time to return to the scenario with which I opened this chapter. You'll recall that teachers at an elementary school were struggling with implementing a district-mandated curriculum change. An initial staff meeting revealed widely varying attitudes about the change, and it ended without an action plan having been agreed on.

The principal called a second meeting and asked for the assistance of an outside facilitator. After introducing the Transition and Development FrameWork, the facilitator asked teachers to place a sticker on the FrameWork to indicate at what stage they were regarding the new literacy approach. The results showed that about 70% of the group placed themselves at the Aware and Acknowledge stages, and 30% were at Acquire and Act.

The facilitator asked if anyone had an explanation for the results. One teacher said, "I think I know what's going on here." She asked those in the Acquire and Act stage to stand. When they did, people began nodding and smiling as it registered that those teachers had been in the first training session, held at the beginning of the previous summer, while the others—the 70%—were in a second session, held later.

Those in the first group were asked to describe their journey from Acknowledge and Accept to Acquire and Act. As they talked, the others looked doubtful and puzzled. "Where did you get that?" someone asked. "It wasn't in the manual."

It quickly became clear that two different trainings had taken place. The first was done by the person who wrote the training manual and who supplemented it with information and explanation based on his own extensive experience. The second training was conducted by someone who did not provide much more than the material in the manual.

People who experienced the first training were made aware of substantial differences between what they had been doing and what the new approach would involve. They emerged from that experience with a strong feeling of acknowledgement and a sense of what they needed to acquire in order to act. The second group, on the other hand, completed their training with the attitude that there was little substantive difference between their former methods and what they were being told to do going forward. Consequently, they modified their teaching approach only slightly.

The principal asked the person who had conducted the first training to come back and retrain all the staff more extensively. Within a month, she noticed a reduction in tension and an increase in collaboration among teachers.

Transition/Development and Partnership

Throughout this book I've been emphasizing that partnership isn't natural or easy. What I mean is that because of the individualistic and competitive culture we find ourselves in, our default setting is to go it alone, to see others as rivals, to be wary of ceding our authority to someone else. We can act otherwise, but only by dint of conscious effort. To say something is unnatural is not to say it's impossible, only that it will initially require more work.

Try an experiment. Write your name with your opposite hand. If you're right-handed, write your name with your left hand, or vice versa.

I'm guessing that performing this experiment made you feel awkward and uncoordinated. I'm betting that it took longer to write your name than it does with your usual hand. But I'm also guessing that you were able to do it, that you produced a signature someone else could read. It might have looked shaky, but it was legible.

Partnership takes longer than a command-control way of operating. Operating in partnership requires taking time for reflection, deliberation, and lots of practice. One value of the FrameWork discussed in this chapter is that by abstracting or isolating the stages of a transition, we are forced to become more self-aware, and that slows us down.

Another thing this FrameWork does is reinforce the truth that awareness of a change is not enough. Someone can be aware of what a change represents, even be personally convinced of the need to change, and still choose not to change.

I began this chapter by asking, "Who do you serve?" I've found that people who won't change are usually in service to themselves. People who operate in partnership, on the other hand, are in service to the mission nand people of the organization.

Think about your own role at the place where you work.

Who do you serve?

Transition and Development FrameWork

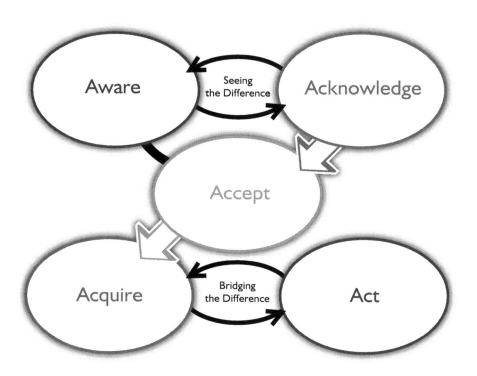

Key Points about Transition and Development FrameWork

- Awareness + Acknowledgement does not always = Acceptance. Often, it results in denial.

- My awareness is usually quite different from others' awareness, so our acknowledgement will be fundamentally different.

- Awareness rarely results in ability, and acceptance makes all the difference.

- Acquire and Acting require feedback loops and continuous monitoring and improvement for any major change in core professional practices and beliefs.

Key Questions

1. What are the Awareness points in my/our current reality? What is my experience and sense making?

2. What differences does that Awareness make for my current assumptions, beliefs, and practices? What do I need to Acknowledge to change?

3. Of all that I need to Acknowledge, what do I Accept to change?

4. What development is needed to Acquire the necessary skills and capacity?

5. How can I continuously improve on my ability to Act, deliver, and perform as needed?

Chapter 5:
Making Decisions

In a mid-sized religious denomination, demographics are changing. The organization's oldest churches are located in the downtown areas of several large cities, where membership is declining. Meanwhile, there is considerable opportunity for expansion in the suburbs, where some congregations are threatening to outgrow their facilities and where members and ministers want to establish new congregations.

Denominational leaders convene a series of meetings to discuss possible changes. They invite ministers, members, local business representatives, and neighbors. Participants brainstorm solutions and come up with several recommendations, none of which involve closing any churches.

Two weeks later, the denomination announces its decision to close three downtown churches and reassign those ministers to existing congregations elsewhere. The pastors they are to replace are told that they will be involved in starting new churches in other areas.

Knowing Your Role

Understanding roles with in any organizational process is critical to the success of your endeavor whether it is in the context of a faith community or even a sports team. If you read the sports page, you're familiar with this exchange. A reporter asks someone from a team that's playing well, "What's the secret of your success this season?" The reply: "We all know our roles."

Sports, like much of modern society, has become increasingly specialized. Years ago, it was not uncommon for football players to "go both ways," that is, to play both offense and defense. These days, going both ways—except, perhaps, at a very small high school—is rare. Now, someone usually plays either offense or defense.

I'm old enough to remember the days in baseball when there were two kinds of pitchers: starters and relievers. Now, any professional team has a starting rotation of five pitchers, plus a couple who can be called on for "middle relief," plus a few "setup" men, and a "closer." Teams also try to carry a mix of right-handed and left-handed pitchers, on the assumption that a right-hander will be more effective against a right-handed batter, and vice versa.

And that's just pitching. Defensively, it's unusual for a starter to play more than one position. It's assumed, for example, that the demands of playing shortstop are sufficiently distinctive that asking a shortstop to play second base would mean a falloff in defensive quality. Offensively, most managers tinker with the batting order, always looking for a better mix of contact hitters and power hitters. Who should bat leadoff? Who should hit cleanup?

And that's just on the field. In the dugout, there's a manager and a bench coach, plus a pitching coach, bullpen coach, and first- and third-base coaches.

And that's just baseball. In football, there's the kickoff team, the punting team, the extra-point team, the field-goal team. There's the prevent defense and the two-minute offense. There's the offensive line coach, the linebackers coach, the special teams coach, the strength coach.

It can all be a bit overwhelming, especially for someone who's not a serious sports fan. In fact, even serious fans often specialize, the task of learning the particulars of a given sport being so demanding that the prospect of keeping up on several is too much for many.

An athletic team is a microcosm of any large organization. As businesses grow, they generate a greater variety of roles. Flow charts and reporting lines are a fact of life in most businesses. So what did that player mean by attributing the team's success to people knowing their roles? And how does that apply to the way other organizations work?

Knowing one's role involves several things. Most important, perhaps, is acceptance. If the manager has designated you for middle relief, it's unproductive to wish you were the closer. Knowing your role means accepting your place in the larger organization. It means trying to become the best at what you do while also helping others become better at what they do.

Seen in this light, being a "role player" is not second-class citizenship. Rather, in a well-functioning organization, everyone is a role player. In other words, everyone recognizes the legitimate division of labor on which successful collectivities operate and accepts his or her place in the grand scheme of things.

And it is the responsibility of Tops and Middles to constantly clarify and describe the roles of all employees, to "Manage When I Must" clearly, consistently, and fairly.

Acceptance doesn't mean stasis, doesn't rule out having aspirations and trying to move up the ladder. After all, most organizations promote their best employees. But knowing your role does mean being able to apply yourself to the task at hand without trying to assume someone else's responsibilities. It means being content to be a part—your part regardless of position, title. or level—of the whole. All of which suggests that engaging in your role also means being able to trust others.

As I've indicated throughout this book, partnership is founded on trust. Operating in partnership necessitates acknowledging other people's abilities—their roles—and assuming they are competent to fulfill those roles, just as they assume you are competent to fulfill yours.

Many of us are well-schooled in the art of trusting ourselves. We resonate with Ralph Waldo Emerson's words: "Trust thyself: Every heart vibrates to that iron string." But we tend to forget the next sentence in Emerson's essay: "Accept the place the divine providence has for you, the society of your contemporaries, the connection of events."

Knowing your role is a balancing act—between an individual initiative and aspiration that fuels innovation and progress, and an acceptance of one's place that acknowledges an interdependence with others.

I've been talking about knowing one's place largely in individual terms: knowing *your* place. There's also a larger context to be considered, one that involves knowing *everyone's* place and determining how the various roles in an organization can function together most efficiently and productively. The roles in decision making need to be clearly defined, communicated, and understood by the participants. That, in a nutshell, is what leaders do, and it's a function that is crucial for effective decision making.

Decision Making as an Exercise in Partnership

To help an organization distinguish among its members' roles and responsibilities, I use the following Decision Making FrameWork.

Figure 9: Decision Making FrameWork

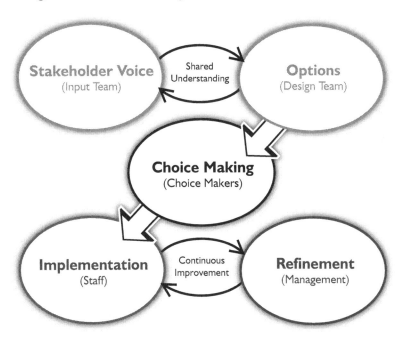

In most organizations I work with, people have a finely tuned sense of how important it is to solicit input from various stakeholders when making decisions. At its worst, that process is motivated merely by a sense of obligation—legal or political. In this regard, people talk about "due diligence." Due diligence is something you better do—or at least go through the motions of doing—to protect yourself.

A more helpful attitude is to see the process of gathering others' input as a valued and important act undertaken to create the best, most informed basis in developing options for making a decision. But even when organizations have the right motives, they can flounder if they fail to recognize the distinctive roles that are necessary for effective decision making in complex organizations. That's where the Decision Making FrameWork comes in.

Effective decision making starts with identifying who has what roles and when a choice must be made. This is followed by mapping the work of many people, operating in partnership across multiple roles. The first group to identify are the Choice Makers, those held accountable for the implications of a choice. Next is the Design Team, organized largely according to knowledge and implementation accountability. The Design Team typically includes operational managers and technical knowledge experts, both internal and external. Finally, there is the Input Team, organized largely according to representation of the stakeholders and constituencies affected by a choice.

In the scenario that opened this chapter, the Input Team involved ministers, members, business representatives, and community members. In a school district facing a major budget change, it might include teachers and school staff, parents, other community members, and perhaps students.

The purpose of the Input Team is to create a shared understanding, an environment in which the most informed decision can be made in partnership and in consultation with the Design Team. The Input Team provides feedback, brainstorming, risk identification, and consultation to the Design Team regarding options being developed for the Choice Makers.

The Design Team's job is to generate options based on information: data, trends, influences, needs. A common exercise for such a group is to conduct a SWOT analysis by determining the organization's strengths, weaknesses, opportunities, and threats. The Design Team's members should be those people who are most familiar with the organization at all levels. In our church scenario, it might consist of ministry directors and the business administrator.

In the Decision Making FrameWork, there is a feedback loop between the Input and Design Teams. The loop reflects the fact that as options are generated, they may be subject to further input. Interaction between the two teams usually leads to deeper thinking and more robust options.

Eventually, of course, the input- and options-generating functions must end and a choice must be made. Here is where I see many organizations go astray.

Common Perils of Making Choices

There are several common mistakes to avoid in choice making. One is not specifying who the Choice Makers are, or making that group too large. That approach can result in a too-many-cooks-spoil-the-broth muddle. This problem often results from the misguided notion that just because stakeholders' suggestions have been solicited, all of them should be involved in making the decision. The fact is that including stakeholders at the input stage does not create an obligation to use all that input or to invest them with choice-making authority.

A better approach is to ask, "Who will be accountable for this choice?" If, down the road, the choice proves to have been unwise, who should get the heat? Where does the buck stop?

A related mistake is to naively commit to consensus. In Chapter 1, I quoted Edwin Olson and Glenda Eoyang, who noted that seeking consensus, while often a worthy goal, can result in a group getting bogged down or settling for less-than-optimal solutions. In my own consulting work, I've found that consensus can be used to abdicate authority, escape accountability, or create a false sense of equality.

As I've stressed before, partnership is not a relationship among equals; it is a relationship of shared leadership across differences in authority. That's why successful partnership depends on distinguishing roles and then coordinating the interaction of people occupying complementary but distinctive roles.

Another error that Choice Makers might make, one I've addressed in previous chapters, is to short-circuit the process by choosing too soon. Partnership takes time. In my experience, options usually cycle between the Input and Design teams about three times. Granted, you don't want that interaction to become an endless loop and an excuse to avoid knuckling down and making a choice. But the greater danger, based on my experience, is for choice makers to act prematurely.

A related misstep is for Choice Makers to insert themselves in the interaction between the Input and Design teams. When leaders ask me what their role should be in that process, I often say it's to welcome, participate, listen, and serve cookies. This role is hard for people accustomed to being in charge. They're not used to sitting in the stands; they want to be out on the field. In some cases I advise leaders to leave the room. Sometimes the mere presence of a leader can squelch interaction.

If Choice Makers are in the room, there are things they can do to signal their role. In a meeting, a Choice Maker frequently will be asked, "What do you think?" The correct answer to that question is, "I'm not here to offer my opinions. I'm here to listen, answer questions, and take notes."

Beyond what one says and doesn't say in a stakeholder meeting, there are other things one can do to reinforce a noninterventionist role. Earlier I discussed the importance of such things as attire and physical position in managing authority. If a stakeholder meeting is taking place on a Saturday morning, a Choice Maker should not show up in a suit. If stakeholders are sitting around a conference table, Choice Makers usually sit to the side.

Choice Makers can even go out of their way to adopt a custodial role. Be the person who dims the lights for a PowerPoint presentation. Be the one who makes coffee or puts out snacks. You don't have to wear an apron, but you can signal in a variety of ways that your role is to serve and be helpful to others for their roles.

A final error, perhaps the most serious one leaders can make, is to solicit input and options, but not take them into account in making a decision. A stakeholder group often includes representatives from outside the organization: clients, vendors, neighborhood residents. Asking people to attend meetings outside their own work schedule and then ignoring their input is insulting. This is the mistake the denominational leaders made in our opening scenario.

Later in this chapter, I'll introduce the use of a Guiding Change document in the Decision Making process. By not stating up front that not closing church facilities was an unacceptable mean, the Choice Makers limited the ability of the Input and Design Teams to do their best and most creative work. In addition, the announcement, whatever the choice might be, needs to clearly show the impact and influence of the Input Team's work on the final decision.

Stated positively, if Choice Makers know their role, then stakeholders will feel energized and empowered to do real work. As a leader, when you've convinced people that your role is confined to observing and listening, they will behave differently. If you conspicuously drop the reins, they'll pick them up.

Partnership is more than due diligence. It means more than satisfying some real or perceived requirement for outside input. Partnership demands a genuine openness to others' ideas and a willingness to change the plan based on their suggestions.

Guiding Change Revisited

I've stressed that Choice Makers should not intrude on the work of the Input or Design teams. But that doesn't mean those groups are left with no guidance or direction. In Chapter 2, I talked at length about how to guide change, and the strategies discussed there provide the preliminary work for the decision-making process described in this chapter. So, before stakeholder meetings commence, Choice Makers will have already determined unacceptable means, and what I've called a Guiding Change document will be in place.

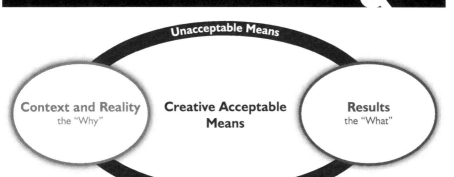

The Guiding Change document is a reference point for both the Input and Design Teams. It describes the end-in-view (though not the means for getting there) and spells out the "not-how": unacceptable means for arriving at the desired end. If the Input or Design Team seems to be getting off track, the guiding change document will pull them back on task.

Which is not to say that a Guiding Change document is carved in stone. It should be considered flexible, subject to amending and refining. Like the U.S. Constitution, a Guiding Change document shouldn't be added to casually, but as with the Constitution, it's possible things will develop that the original framers didn't anticipate, and an amendment will be appropriate.

Implementation: Making it Happen

What's the greatest threat to implementing a choice? It's that those charged with implementation won't actually enact the plan. Or, rather, that they will implement poorly by slowing it down, ignoring it and letting it languish until it goes away. When Tops make executive decisions and deliver them to Middles with little prelude, process, or previous involvement, those choices stand a good chance of never being fully realized.

Good parents understand this dynamic. Consider the parents of two families. The first announces to the children at breakfast that he's decided to implement a schedule for household chores. Beds will be made and rooms picked up daily. Wastebaskets will be emptied weekly. Dishwashing will be divided into the following tasks: clearing the table, washing, rinsing, drying, and putting away. The kids will rotate through those tasks according to a set schedule. And so on and so on.

The second parent gets her children together and says, "There are a lot of things to do around the house to keep it running smoothly. It seems to me that we've all been a bit haphazard in how we do things, and I wonder if we can come up with a better system. Why don't you kids talk it over and see if you can generate some ideas. I've made a list of household tasks that I thought of. You can start with that, but you might come up with other things. What I'd like is some kind of schedule for who does what and when. I'll be in the family room if you have any questions."

Which household is more likely to see improvement?

As a Top, unless you're prepared to implement all phases of the major decisions your organization makes, you need to involve people in the decision-making process. If you always manage and never partner, you'll arrive at decisions quickly but will run the risk that the people you depend on to put those decisions into practice will drag their feet, or go through the motions, or even actively sabotage things.

Implementation is rarely cut and dried. It can involve a host of considerations: targets, measures, resource allocation, etc. Because of the strategic importance of implementation, it's advisable to have people who will be involved in it participate on the Design Team. If implementers have participated in previous steps in the process, they're more likely to be committed to a decision than if it's been sprung on them out of the blue.

Refinement: Making it Better

When an organization has been through a long decision-making process and has finally implemented a plan, the tendency is immediately to turn attention to the next decision. That approach would be fine if every idea were perfect and every implementation went exactly as planned. The reality, though, is that even the best process cannot predict every outcome.

In the Decision Making FrameWork, just as there is a feedback loop between the Input and Design Teams, there is structured interaction between the Implementation and Refinement stages of decision making. I call this feedback loop continuous improvement. Both loops are based on the same assumption: that coming up with specifics—whether options or implementation steps—means communicating with other groups involved in the process. One difference between the two loops is that the first one, the process of creating a shared understanding, must eventually come to an end. Continuous improvement, on the other hand, is much more open-ended, and the refining process could continue indefinitely.

Using the Decision Making FrameWork

By now it shouldn't need repeating: Partnership takes time. Using the Decision Making FrameWork described in this chapter involves commitment to a process that will usually extend over a period of weeks or months. Obviously, not every decision an organization makes can be subjected to that process. Adhering to a philosophy of "Partner When WE Should **&** Manage" When I Must, then, means judging when to use this FrameWork. That decision should be guided by several criteria.

Managing is the better option when...	Partnership is the better option when...
• time is limited	• time is open or flexible
• a choice is clear	• a choice is not clear
• an end can be easily determined	• an end is in view but not determined

Giving Credit: How the Buck Got Here

I should say a word about terminology. I've appropriated Barry Oshry's classification—Tops, Middles, and Bottoms—because it's a convenient shorthand for describing the three major levels in organizations. Oshry's differentiations are both structural and situational. One can be a structural Top such as a CEO, but in the presence of the Board of Directors might be a Middle, and at times feel quite like a Bottom.

Using Oshry's terms is a way of reinforcing two complementary truths about organizational life:

- Hierarchy is necessary and good.

- Organizations depend on people occupying different roles.

There is a danger, however, that Oshry's distinctions could be seen as implying a value judgment. In Chapter 3, I cited George Lakoff and Mark Johnson's observation about orientational metaphors: that high status is up and low status is down. I hope I've made it clear in this book that one's place in an organizational flow chart says nothing about that person's worth. I also hope it's clear that partnership means a softening of hierarchy. In a given circumstance, I've suggested, a Top might behave like a Bottom by serving cookies. Engaging in partnership means being flexible, fitting one's behavior to the situation at hand.

Partnering when you can also means giving credit where credit is due. Even loyal fans of a particular football team might be hard-pressed to name the interior linemen, who usually labor in obscurity, whereas they're likely to know the running backs and quarterback. In a postgame interview after rushing for 150 yards, the fullback is not just being modest when he says, "The offensive line kept opening holes all day. I just ran through them." Similarly, the quarterback who passed for 350 yards and three touchdowns might well say, "My line gave me plenty of time to throw, and the receivers made some great catches."

President Harry Truman popularized the expression, "The buck stops here," and had a sign with that inscription on his desk in the White House. By saying the buck stops here, Truman meant that he accepted responsibility for whatever made it to his desk. He would not make excuses or pass responsibility on to someone else.

But how did the "buck" get to Truman's desk? Only through the work of countless other people, many of them operating out of the limelight.

Good leaders accept responsibility. They take the heat when there's heat to be taken. They don't resort to vagaries like "Mistakes were made." They own up to things.

But good leaders also acknowledge the work of others. They recognize the important roles that others play, and they applaud a job well done.

Role Playing: The Big Picture

We all have our roles to play in an organization and it's important to keep the bigger picture in perspective. It gives meaning to our work. The feeling of being a mere cog in a great machine can have vastly different connotations depending on how one views the machine.

Consider this story about a traveler in the Middle Ages who happened upon a construction site. She approached a worker and asked what he was doing.

"I'm cutting stone," he replied.

She asked the same question of a second man.

"I'm mixing mortar," he said.

Finally, she went up to a third man and asked, "What are you doing?"

"I'm building a cathedral," he said.

Cathedral construction depends on a variety of skills. A stone cutter needs to know his role and to concentrate on doing the best job he can. He doesn't have to worry about how and when a particular stone will be laid. That's the job of the general contractor, who must have a vision for how each stage in the construction process should progress.

The stone cutter can get along all right by just turning out stones that are cut to the proper specifications. But how much more meaningful his work will be if he sees it as part of a larger effort that will one day result in a thing of great beauty.

What are you building?

Decision Making FrameWork

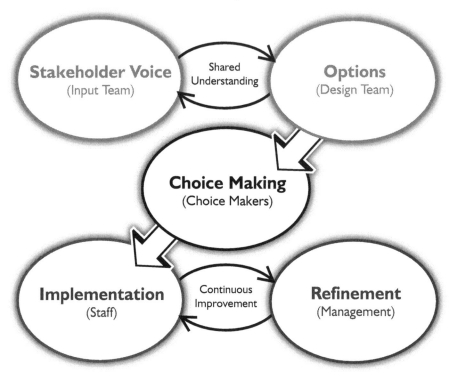

Key Points about Decision Making FrameWork

- The Decision Making FrameWork is used primarily for mapping roles, responsibilities, relationships, and process.

- Choice Makers are those accountable for the implications of the choice.

- Design Team is organized around knowledge, and Input Team around representation.

- Design Team should provide two options to Choice Makers that each satisfy the conditions and parameters of the Guiding Change document.

Key Questions

1. Who will be accountable if the choice made is the best, or worst, ever made?

2. Is the end determined or in-view? If determined, do not use FrameWork.

3. When must a choice be made and implementation occur?

4. Who are the real stakeholders affected by a possible choice and change?

5. What is the process flow of meetings and work to achieve the time frame?

Chapter 6:
Leveraging the Strengths of
Personality

Ted, the Communications Director, had spent hours preparing. His PowerPoint presentation was meticulously organized and flawlessly delivered. Each slide had one major point, and the crisp black font on a white background made things easily visible from the back of the room.

Although he felt like the presentation had gone well, when Ted switched off the projector, he sensed that the audience was unimpressed and disconnected. Questions were perfunctory, and the general mood was skeptical. It looked like Ted's proposal wasn't going to get very far. Doubt began to rise in Ted's mind, and stories about himself and his audience began to form.

Human Difference

It's an observation at once commonplace and profound: People are different. Perhaps no issue is more consequential for an organization's success than how it deals with its members' differences. Is human variability leveraged for its creative potential, or does organizational culture and practice allow people's differences to thwart positive change?

People differ in every way imaginable—physically, mentally, socially, psychologically. Although one's genetic inheritance influences one's personality and what sort of person one becomes, even siblings may exhibit a wide range of differences. Most people are capable of varied responses in a given situation, but we all have innate tendencies and preferences—certain ways of processing information and reacting to stimuli that make up our individual personality. We acknowledge those differences all the time:

"I'm just not a morning person."

"My brother is the party animal in the family."

"I hate talking to people when I can't look at them."

"She's good at seeing the big picture."

"I always cry at sad movies."

"He can tell what I'm thinking just by looking at me."

"I'd rather see a picture of something than read about it."

We usually use the term personality to refer, as the word suggests, to a particular person: to what makes an individual distinctively himself or herself. But it's also true that a group of people can take on a distinctive "personality" if its members share certain tendencies or preferences. And sometimes, a whole organization or system can have a distinctive identity. To help people become more aware of their individual and group personality differences, I use the following Four Color View FrameWork.

Figure 10: Four Color View FrameWork

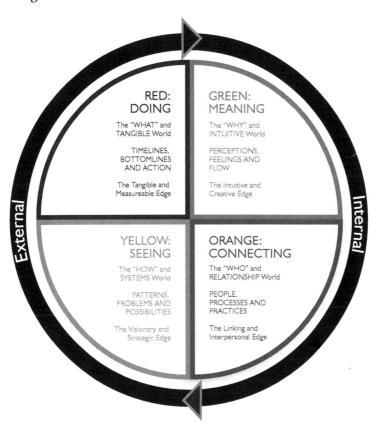

The four-color schema of classifying personality is based on the work of Dr. Carol Ritberger. The scheme is symbolic in that colors are used to differentiate personality types and tendencies rather than to reflect color preferences. And the colors don't have anything to do with certain traditional associations, such as red = angry or yellow = cowardly.

In the Four Color View FrameWork, if your dominant personality color is Red, that means you approach matters logically. You favor quick decisions and thrive in competitive situations. By contrast, Greens are intuitive. They approach matters artistically and are good at seeing things holistically. For Oranges, the relational dimension is important. They excel at anticipating how a particular decision will affect others. Yellows see the big picture. They're good at imagining different possibilities and seeing both the forest and the trees.

The Four Color View is based on the assumption that each of us has a personality type—a set of preferences and tendencies for how we think, feel, respond, and behave. Having a preference doesn't mean that you're locked into a particular type. We can and do act "outside of type," but doing so requires more conscious intention—and often more energy—than does acting according to our inherent personality type.

This is not unlike the earlier example of signing your name with your "opposite" hand. Most people can produce a legible signature that way, but it doesn't look like their usual one. Furthermore, signing your name 50 times with the opposite hand would take much longer and leave that hand much more tired than would executing your signature normally.

In the same way, if you're the sort of person who gravitates toward a quiet corner during a party, that doesn't mean you're unable to approach strangers and introduce yourself. But you may have to force yourself to do so, and the process will take more out of you than it would for someone who's naturally gregarious. Indeed, that person may find energizing what you find draining—and vice versa.

The Red Personality

Reds are pragmatic, realistic, no-nonsense types. They thrive in environments where rules and expectations are clearly delineated and everyone knows their place. Reds are uncomfortable with ambiguity, preferring that things be clearly spelled out. In a brainstorming session, a Red wants to know what the outcome of the session will be. Reds are highly conscious of time and using it productively. They become impatient if they think others are wasting time. Reds don't want to hear how hard other people are working; they want to know when the job will be done.

Reds are concrete rather than abstract thinkers. They like to be in control—of people and situations. They prefer detailed job descriptions and clear lines of authority, and they don't like surprises. They're detail-oriented, and they thrive in competitive environments.

On the minus side, Reds can be experienced as stubborn and domineering. On the plus side, they are productive, loyal, and consistent. Reds are bottom-line, let's-get-it-done people.

The Yellow Personality

Yellows lend themselves to the prefix "self": self-reliant, self-motivated, self-confident, self-starting. They approach problems intellectually and have a strong desire to learn new things, with a need to understand how things work, which can lead them to challenge the status quo. Yellows enjoy thinking of new and innovative ways of doing things.

Yellows operate from a strong set of internal values and are not shy about challenging anyone or anything that conflicts with their beliefs. They're often seen as nonconformists, and they thrive in situations where they enjoy autonomy and independence. They enjoy being looked to as experts. In groups, they serve as gadflies and provocateurs.

On the minus side, Yellows can be critical, skeptical, and judgmental. They often get bogged down in planning rather than executing. On the plus side, Yellows hold themselves and others to high standards. They are visionaries who excel at charting a new course. Yellows are let's-do-it-better people.

The Orange Personality

Oranges are caretakers, often putting others' needs ahead of their own. They're community-oriented and like to be involved in activities with an obvious humanitarian outcome. Oranges make good administrators because they read other people well and are able to enlist others' cooperation and support. Oranges like being information hubs and are good communicators.

In groups, Oranges are happiest when everyone participates, and they'll make an effort to draw out more reticent members. Although Oranges work well in groups, if they feel let down by the rest of the team, they can react strongly.

On the minus side, Oranges can be worriers and emotionally vulnerable. They might clam up in a competitive situation. On the plus side, Oranges are sensitive, thoughtful, and cooperative. Oranges are let's-all-get-along people.

The Green Personality

Greens are imaginative, intuitive, and creative. They thrive on change and are easily bored by anything they think is stagnant or dull. Like Yellows, Greens have little patience with the status quo, but unlike Yellows, they tend to be non-confrontational. Greens dislike conflict and will try to adapt their own style in the interests of promoting harmony.

Greens love to brainstorm. They are cheerleaders who enjoy encouraging others to do their best. They're passionate about what they believe in. Greens are able to see the big picture and are good at helping others see it too. They're not bound by the clock.

On the minus side, Greens can be gullible and naïve. They might appear flighty and oversensitive. On the plus side, Greens are idealistic, optimistic, inspirational, and flexible. They inspire others to greater achievement, and they help keep groups interacting smoothly. Greens are let's-enjoy-ourselves people.

The Power of Personality

Observing that people are different takes no special insight. What's challenging is being able to assess your own and others' personalities and then figuring out how to mesh individual differences to accomplish a particular purpose. And what's especially challenging—and important—is being able to adapt your personality style to meet the needs of a specific situation.

The scenario that started this chapter is an example of what can happen when styles are misaligned. The PowerPoint was created by Ted, who is a Red. It was straightforward and logical, short on ornamentation and long on practicality. Unfortunately for Ted, the audience was mostly made up of Greens and Oranges. They would have responded more favorably to a presentation with colors and images, one that made an emotional as well as an intellectual appeal. And indeed they did react that way a week later, after Ted had been exposed to the Four Color View and had revised his presentation for an audience quite different from himself.

The scenario illustrates a point I made earlier, that groups as well as individuals have styles: preferred ways of processing information and making decisions. A group's style might reflect its most dominant member(s) or might simply be an indication of a majority preference.

For example, in a group made up mostly of Greens, meetings may rarely start on time. Such a group will be less concerned with sticking to an agenda than would one whose members are predominantly Reds.

A team whose style is mainly Orange may function better if meetings include food. In an Orange group, a reticent person will have a hard time being a silent observer because others will keep trying to draw him out.

Describing a group as Orange or Green doesn't mean it functions only in ways consistent with that style. Just as individuals can consciously adapt their style to fit a given situation, so too can groups adjust their behavior by acting outside type.

For example, Mark, who is an introverted Orange, prefers to listen for quite awhile before contributing in a group setting. He takes longer to process information than most other group members, but when he speaks it's often to great effect. Mark has a way of summarizing a discussion succinctly and objectively. He often says things like, "I heard Betty say . . . and I heard José say . . . ." Mark sometimes states his own views, but he's also likely to say something like, "It seems to me that if we pursue the first option, we'll probably face X. On the other hand, if we go with the second option, Y is the most likely result."

In a group where members like everyone to participate, people will be better off not trying to get Mark talking before he's ready. If they're sensitive

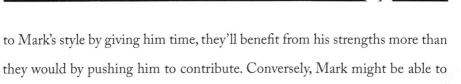

to Mark's style by giving him time, they'll benefit from his strengths more than they would by pushing him to contribute. Conversely, Mark might be able to perform a valuable service by acting outside type if he sees the discussion getting off track and interjects an early comment that pulls people back on topic.

Making Colors Work

There are two lessons to be drawn from the Four Color View FrameWork. The first is awareness: Know yourself and get to know those around you. Learn about your strengths and weaknesses, and maximize what you're good at. The second lesson is flexibility: Learn to determine when it's worth the effort to move outside your dominant type and instead adopt a less dominant personality type.

One misuse of the Four Color View is what I call Rogerism, named for someone I used to work with. Roger liked to circulate. He'd watch what you were doing for awhile, then remark, "You know, you're really good at that. I don't know what it is, but I've just never been able to get the hang of what you're doing." The fact is, Roger was lazy, and there appeared to be little that he "got the hang of." Admitting his alleged weaknesses was just a way to avoid responsibility.

At the other extreme was Shirley. She was such a people pleaser that she tried to take on things that would have been better left to others. Driven by a can-do attitude, Shirley too often found herself in over her head or spread too thin. She would have been more effective by admitting her weaknesses and letting other people do what she wasn't as good at.

Of course, sometimes one doesn't have the luxury of letting someone else do it. Recently a household project called for me to reach between the wall and refrigerator and drive a screw with my right hand. I'm left-handed, but I've done enough work around the house to have encountered similar situations in the past, and I've developed sufficient facility with my right hand to get by.

Let's say you're in a group that's always been facilitated by Martina—a Red. People have gotten used to starting and ending on time, following an agenda, avoiding small talk, and concluding with a list of responsibilities. One day, Martina goes home sick. Someone else will have to lead the meeting.

You're an Orange. You like meetings where people bring treats, the schedule is relaxed, and the atmosphere is informal. Today, though, people won't be expecting that kind of thing. You've been on this team from the beginning, and you're the logical person to take over for Martina. Can you step outside your comfort zone?

Using Personality Awareness to Communicate Effectively

Once you've made a judgment about someone else's personal style, you can make a conscious effort to communicate in a way that will get that person's attention and elicit a positive response. Here are some suggestions for effective communication based on your audience's color.

Reds

- Know what you're going to say before you start talking.
- Be confident and assertive.
- Stick to the facts and to the point. Don't ramble.

- Tell before you show (auditory first, visual second).

- Stress how what you're presenting can be put to immediate use.

- Expect frank, blunt responses.

Here are some statements to get a Red's attention:

"Let's get to the bottom line."

"Here's what the research says."

"Let's not reinvent the wheel."

"Here's what has worked before."

"The first step is __. The second step is __."

Yellows

- Don't equivocate. State things honestly and forthrightly.

- Focus on the big picture.

- Use language that stimulates divergent thinking.

- Present possibilities rather than offering conclusions.

- When possible, present information in writing first.

- Resist the temptation to finish someone's sentences.

Here are some statements and questions to get a Yellow's attention:

"What's wrong with this picture?"

"Let me bounce this idea off you."

"What's your take on the situation?"

"We need someone to take charge of this project."

"What do you think our strategy should be?"

Oranges

- Be courteous. Avoid offensive language.

- Use your own personal experiences to illustrate a point.

- Be conscious of body language—yours and your listener's.

- Say something positive before offering a criticism.

- Give sincere compliments.

- Be clear about what you expect.

Here are some statements and questions to get an Orange's attention:

"Can you help me understand this?"

"You have my word on it."

"What would make you more comfortable?"

"How are you feeling about this?"

"I'm having trouble getting through to _____. Would you talk to her?"

Greens

- Use imagistic, metaphorical language.

- Provide options.

- Let your voice reflect your commitment and passion.

- Ask open-ended questions.

- Address people by name.

- Share your own ideals and dreams.

Here are some statements and questions to get a Green's attention:

"Let's brainstorm to see if we can come up with something different."

"What new and exciting things are going on with you?"

"What's your intuition telling you?"

"Paint me a picture."

"What would you do in this situation?"

Personality and Partnership

As I've stressed throughout this book, partnership depends on communication. The Four Color View FrameWork provides a way to facilitate effective communication by identifying the most common ways that people process information.

If someone describes another person as a great communicator, what do you assume about that person? Certainly communicating means talking: telling, describing, illustrating, persuading. So effective communicators are those who use words well. But communication involves more than words, and people who are good at it also pay attention to its nonverbal dimension. I talked about some nonverbal forms of communication in Chapter 3 when I gave suggestions for amplifying and softening authority. What you wear or where you sit or stand can have a lot to do with how you are perceived.

But communication isn't just about you. Effective communicators are good listeners and observers, and they're able to adjust both the verbal and nonverbal components of their message to a person's or audience's needs and preferences. But how do you know what those preferences are? More specifically, how do you know if your audience—whether a person or a group—is Red, Yellow, Orange, or Green?

When listening to others talk, pay attention to what kinds of language they use. For example, if someone regularly uses variations of the word *think* (e.g., "Here's what I *think*" or "Here are my *thoughts*"), chances are that person is a Red or Yellow, personalities that process information cognitively. Conversely, if someone tends to say things like, "This is how I *feel*" or "I'm *feeling* like we need to consider other options," it's likely that person is an Orange or Green.

In Chapter 3, I cited Deborah Tannen's distinction between report talk and rapport talk. The former is informational and objective; the latter is relational and subjective. Reds and Yellows are more comfortable with report talk, Oranges and Greens with rapport talk.

Nonverbal behavior can also provide clues about personality. When talking and listening, Reds and Yellows tend to touch their head—rubbing their chin, wiping their eyes, tugging on an ear. Greens and Oranges, on the other hand, are likely to put a hand to their chest or rub their shoulders.

Partnership depends on an awareness of and sensitivity to others—their strengths, weaknesses, tendencies, and preferences. The Four Color View Framework is a helpful way to assess and understand our preferences, and it provides a scheme for talking about your own and others' standard

operating procedures.

For example, in looking at your schedule, you might say to yourself, "I'll have to be Red today" or "I know I have to raise my Green." If you're a Green facing a Red day, you might need to get extra sleep the night before.

In a group that displays a distinct color tendency, it's helpful to ask questions that focus on a different quadrant. For example, a Red group might need to be asked, "If we move forward, what is your vision of what we are working towards?" That's a question that would not naturally occur to Reds as easily as it would for an Green. Conversely, an Orange group might benefit from being asked, "If we move forward, what is our action plan?" Greens might need to be prompted to think about how something will be accomplished, whereas Yellows may need to be asked who will be most affected by a particular course of action they favor.

The Four Color View Framework is also useful for strategizing at the system level. For example, my organization, Teamworks International, does a lot of work with school districts. We're based in Minnesota, where districts are able to initiate levies and referendums, whereby taxpayers in the district vote on whether to accept additional assessments—beyond the portion of their property taxes that goes to the local school district—in order to fund public education.

One year we analyzed the success of levy and referendum efforts by considering the color preferences implicit in a school district's public statements and appeals. We found that failures were primarily Green-Orange. Those efforts emphasized who the money would benefit—the kids and the community—and why the extra funds were needed. That message did not appeal to the majority of taxpayers. What worked much better were levy-referendum appeals that not only talked about why and who but clearly articulated what the needs were and how the money would be spent to address those needs.

Another thing we've learned is that at the group and system level, most disagreements center on how something will be done. Many groups spend most of their energy arguing about how (a solution and problem-solving orientation) without having adequately considered and reached a shared understanding of the what, why, and who. An effective dialogue process, especially for boards and executive teams, is to focus a critical conversation on the elements of what (Red), why (Green), and who (Orange) top develop a shared understanding before moving to the how (Yellow) and ending with an action plan.

Ultimately, the purpose of identifying preferences with the Four Color View Framework is not to achieve greater self-understanding but rather to help answer the question, "What does our work together need us to be, say, and do?" Partnership necessitates a shift from focusing on the individual to concentrating on the group, from me-reflection to we-reflection. If we collectively need a dose of Red and no one is providing that, then I'll take on a Red role—even if that's not my preferred or natural style. If our group doesn't naturally ask who questions, then we'll need to make a special effort to do that.

If we're honest, most of us would admit to sometimes thinking, "The world would be a better place if other people were more like me." But in our more clear-headed moments, we realize that a one-color world wouldn't work. We need each other—in all our variety and contrariness. As Carol Ritberger puts it, "The paradox of our human existence is that we all treasure personal independence and count on personal interdependence. Management's challenge is to understand the distinctively individual motivations and contributions of each personality color and blend them into a tapestry of productive achievement."

I hope you are becoming part of a beautiful, multicolored tapestry.

Four Color View FrameWork

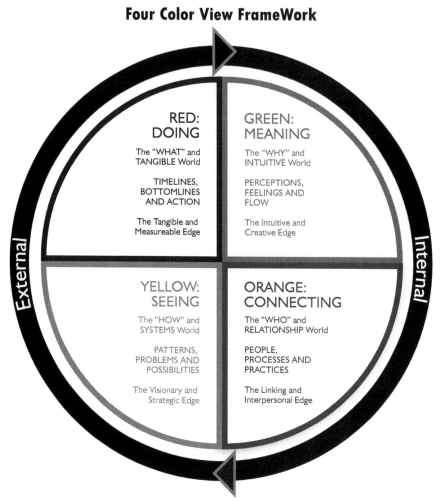

Key Points about Four Color View FrameWork

- All people have elements of all four colors in their Color Personality profile.
- All people can operate out of their dominant personality type, although it takes focus, energy, and intention.
- The FrameWork can be used in many ways: as an instant assessment tool, a communications strategy tool, and a conversation tool.

Key Questions

1. What is my dominant Color Personality type?

2. When interacting with others, what are their dominant types?

3. What type best serves the needs of the organization and others? What will it take for me to provide that type? If I am unable, who else can more easily assist?

4. In a tense conversation, what color is missing? Ask questions in that arena.

5. In a group that is unproductive, what color type is overly present, and what color type is missing? What structures, practices, and roles will help provide a more balanced use of personality strengths?

Conclusion: Intentional Choice

Partnership is not new. In business (Sears and Roebuck, Hewlett and Packard), in entertainment (Laurel and Hardy, Luci and Desi), in crime (Bonnie and Clyde), in crime fighting (Batman and Robin), there is a long tradition illustrating that success can be increased when individuals combine efforts.

But although long-standing, the practice of partnership is not a default setting for most of us. As I've suggested throughout this book, our individualistic and competitive nature reinforces the notion that we rise and fall largely on our own efforts. Entrusting our interests to others, deferring to a group, relinquishing control—these behaviors can seem second-best in an environment where individual achievement is valorized.

We don't get much help in experiencing partnership's potential from the institutions where we spend most of our time prior to entering the workplace. Schools have lab partners and group projects, but few teachers and schools demonstrate the skills, beliefs, and experiences of partnership with their students. As a result, partnership can end up being an adult developmental experience rather than a youth experience. This is beginning to change in schools where life and career skills such as problem solving, higher-order thinking, collaboration, etc. are being integrated into the classroom. Still, many youth experience the fruits of partnership primarily through school-related activities: athletics, performing groups, clubs, and so forth. And some people continue those extracurricular pursuits as adults.

What we experience through these kinds of activities can be among the most powerful influences on our development. Ask a retiree to describe her first job and you might get mostly generalities. But ask her about playing on her high school volleyball team and you might be amazed at the detail of her recollections and the enduring strength of her feelings.

Partnership: A Recapitulation

In this closing chapter, I want to reinforce several fundamental truths about partnership. Reading this conclusion isn't a substitute for reading the whole book, but I hope it helps highlight some of what I've tried to explain throughout.

1. Partnership is based on trust in the competence of self & others.

You can't partner with people you think are not up to the job. Interestingly, I've found that when you communicate—either overtly or covertly—that you believe in someone's ability, that person will usually rise to the occasion and may even surprise you.

In The Inner Game of Tennis, Tim Gallwey, a tennis instructor, describes the typical approach to teaching the game. Traditional instruction usually begins with how to grip the racket, then might cover placement and movement of the feet when hitting a forehand, followed by executing the forehand itself: the position of the arm during takeaway, contact, and follow-through. Eventually, the teacher will take up the backhand and serve, followed in due course by specialized shots: the drop, the lob, the cut. Advanced students might receive lessons in topspin and backspin, analyzing an opponent's weaknesses, and overall strategy.

The conventional approach to tennis instruction, says Gallwey, is based on an assumption of ignorance. The teacher presumes that a beginning student knows nothing and must be taught everything. Indeed, that's how Gallwey practiced his craft for many years. One day, however, he decided to try something different. He told a new student, someone who'd never even held a racket, to watch him hit ten forehands. The student's task was simply to observe and to form a visual image of the forehand shot. Gallwey hit his ten forehands, then told the student, "Let your body imitate the forehand as well as it can."

There was no instruction about grip, stance, takeaway, follow-through, shoulder vs. elbow vs. wrist—just a demonstration. Gallwey was making an important, and unusual, assumption about his student: that he already knew something about tennis but didn't know that he knew. Based on what by any conventional definition would be considered minimal instruction—indeed, non-instruction—Gallwey's student grabbed a racket, bounced a tennis ball, and hit a very creditable forehand.

The poet Kenneth Koch had a similar insight about teaching young children to write poetry. He decried the "condescension toward children's minds and abilities in regard to poetry" in most textbooks. Rather than assuming that elementary students know nothing about writing poetry, Koch had them read "adult" poems by William Blake, John Donne, Walt Whitman, and other major poets. The children were instructed to take a feature of the model poem and construct one of their own using that technique. The results were "better than most of those in elementary-school textbooks . . . serious, deep, honest, lyrical, and formally inventive."

What's true of individuals is also true of groups. Partnership means assuming that an organization itself is competent and worthy of trust, that the ingredients for improvement are already there. The role of a leader—coach, teacher, supervisor, manager—is to recognize that competence, bring it to the fore, and leverage it for the collective good.

2. Partnership is not an alternative to hierarchy but a different view of how hierarchy in a human organization works.

It's important to note that in both of the instructional settings cited above, a traditional hierarchy was maintained. Neither Tim Gallwey nor Kenneth Koch gave up his role as teacher. However, both implicitly redefined the relationship between teacher and student by changing their assumptions and expectations. By treating their beginning students as competent, these teachers drew from them a level of proficiency that others would have found unexpected.

Partnership does not dissolve hierarchy. In a partnering organization, there will be Tops, Middles, and Bottoms. There will be supervision and lines of reporting. There will be employee evaluations, promotions, and demotions.

But in a partnering organization, there will also be flexibility and fluidity. There will be a recognition that power and authority can be shared without threatening their existence. There will be an acknowledgement that in a given situation, a Top can become a Middle or Bottom. There will be a willingness by people at different levels to entrust their self-interest to each other in the service of shared objectives.

Partnering is respectful of hierarchy. But it's also respectful of others' abilities. Partnership means being alert to opportunities for something other than an automatic appeal to traditional expressions of power and authority. It means being able to recognize partnership moments—like the one experienced by the basketball coach in the movie Hoosiers.

3. Partnership maximizes human potential.

When I went to school, learning arithmetic and mathematics followed a predictable pattern. The teacher would introduce a problem, then describe and illustrate the proper procedure for solving it. We students would practice a certain number of problems using the strategy we'd been taught. Success was marked by one's ability to employ consistently the prescribed technique, which math teachers call an algorithm.

What's significant about the process I've described is that the nouns are singular: procedure, strategy, technique, algorithm. Traditional mathematics instruction was based on the assumption that there is one best way to solve problems and that everyone should be taught that way of doing things.

Today, math teachers are likely to introduce more than one way of conceptualizing and solving a problem. Their instruction is based on the assumption that students have different learning styles and preferences, and that if there is more than one route to the same destination, people will benefit from being able to try different routes and discover which work best for them.

Many educators have accepted the notion, first advanced by Howard Gardner, that people have different forms of intelligence. Indeed, some lists of "multiple intelligences" include as many as nine: logical-mathematical, spatial, linguistic, bodily-kinesthetic, musical, interpersonal, intrapersonal, naturalistic, existential-moral.

One advantage of partnership is that it allows the most appropriate abilities or intelligences to emerge in a given situation. A person committed to partnership recognizes that someone else's way of thinking might be superior to his or her own for solving a particular problem or advancing a particular initiative.

4. Partnership means adopting a different attitude toward time.

As I noted in chapter 6, people differ in how they use time. Reds are schedule and agenda oriented, whereas Greens are more comfortable with letting a focus emerge on its own. In a group dominated by Reds, meetings will always start promptly; among Greens, that will never happen.

But although individual differences regarding time are apparent, there are certain cultural assumptions that form a backdrop for all our interactions. Americans think of time as linear, divisible, and quantifiable: something that can be spent, saved, or wasted—just like money. Indeed, one of our catch phrases asserts that "time is money," a conviction that puts a premium on efficiency and speed. Combine that attitude with a competitive bent, and almost any activity—even one that might be classified as leisure—can be put on the clock. Do you like crossword puzzles? Did you know there is an annual event where enthusiasts compete to see who can complete puzzles the fastest?

Cultural assumptions and values about time conspire to create workplace environments that privilege speed and efficiency. In such an atmosphere, any activity that appears to result in "wasting" time is suspect. Yet the fact is that some things shouldn't be rushed, and partnership is one of those things. For that reason, a commitment to partnership means giving people the time they need—to plan, to research, to discuss, to reconsider, to fine-tune.

To be sure, time can be abused; there is such a thing as procrastination. And it's also the case that time can run out; there will always be deadlines. But if deadlines are adequately anticipated and resources effectively deployed, people can be given the time to make partnership work. Making that happen, though, requires foresight, effort, and commitment.

5. Partnership means a willingness to change your mind and the plan.

Ask people what makes a good leader and many will mention decisiveness. In discussions of political candidates, it's common to hear voters say approvingly, "I always know where she stands." Conversely, a candidate who's accused of "flip-flopping" on an issue had better come up with a convincing explanation.

But a narrow view of decisiveness does a disservice to both leaders and followers. For the fact is that good leaders are not cavalier dictators. Good leaders draw on the wisdom and expertise of others. Indeed, good leaders excel at bringing out the best in those around them. And good leaders sometimes change their minds.

Partnership is a relationship that involves Tops, Middles, and Bottoms working together for the common good. When people partner, they commit themselves to a process of interaction that is likely to yield greater clarity and utility as it proceeds. Such a dynamic means that an initial formulation or position or plan might prove inferior to one that emerges from the forge of partnership. And when that happens, the participants must be willing to say, "The new idea is better. We're changing course."

The adjective "two-faced" is pejorative. People who are two-faced are hypocritical, deceitful, double-dealing. Yet the month of January is named for the Roman god Janus, who is depicted with two faces. Poised at the beginning of a new year, January looks two ways: back at the year completed, forward to the year ahead.

To be Janus-like, then, is to be a visionary—drawing on the lessons of the past and alert to the possibilities of the future. We mere mortals cannot have Janus's two faces, but we can, through partnership, see both fore and aft. We can use each other's vision to chart a course we would never discover alone.

6. Partnership is an ongoing commitment, not a one-time experiment.

As you know by now, my mantra is, "Partner When WE Should & Manage When I Must." And my conviction, based on years of working with people in all kinds of organizations, is that opportunities for partnership are numerous. Furthermore, I'm convinced that partnership works best when it achieves "critical mass"—that is, when it's perceived not as an aberration or anomaly but as the preferred way of doing things.

If you've always operated by command-control, or if you work where most people function that way, an announcement that everyone is suddenly going to start partnering likely will be greeted with suspicion. And if partnership is perceived as a style of convenience, suitable only for low-stakes decisions, then it won't work even in those limited situations.

Partnership works best when it's the default setting, when alternatives to it call for justification. There will be situations that demand an executive decision, and as long as leaders are clear about defining those occasions, a prevailing ethos of partnership can continue unthreatened. But if Middles and Bottoms become confused about what's expected of them, or if partnership is only trotted out when not much is at stake, then an organization's potential for collective wisdom and action will never be realized.

One of humankind's greatest achievements is vaccines. Some diseases that once sickened or killed millions of people can be avoided by getting inoculated. And some of those inoculations are permanent—if you get the shot or series of shots, you're protected for life. But getting vaccinated is not a guarantee of lifelong health nor a substitute for ongoing activity: eating a balanced diet, getting regular exercise, avoiding risky behavior.

Partnership is not a vaccine. Partnership is a diet, an exercise, a regular behavior. Furthermore, just as people interested in maintaining their physical health benefit from an annual check-up, so too do those committed to partnership profit from asking themselves, at least once a year, "What am I doing to foster partnership rather than isolation?"

One thing I recommend to groups I work with is an annual "spring cleaning." I urge them to look at their beliefs, words, and actions and make a judgment: What do we want to keep, and what should we throw out? What can be retained as is, and what needs fixing or cleaning up?

A Final Thought

Perhaps the greatest mystery of human life is that we are all individuals, utterly unique, and yet we are intrinsically social creatures. There may be no more dramatic moment in all of literature than when Robinson Crusoe sees a footprint in the sand of his deserted island. Readers know that henceforth everything will be different.

In a modern uninhabited island story, the 2000 movie Cast Away, Chuck Noland, a FedEx productivity analyst played by Tom Hanks, washes up on an island after the plane he's in crashes at sea. During an initial attempt to make a fire, Noland cuts his hand. Depressed and on the verge of despair, he grabs several objects salvaged from FedEx packages that washed up along with him and flings them away in anger. One of these is a volleyball, perhaps as useless an object as could be imagined for a castaway. Later, Noland retrieves the ball, notices his bloody handprint on it, adds features to create a face, and gives the ball a name. It is Nolan's "conversations" with "Wilson" that enable him to maintain his sanity and resolve, and the film's most emotional moment is when, in the homemade craft with which Nolan finally leaves the island, Wilson is swept overboard and lost.

We need others, and if we're deprived of human contact, we may even resort to imbuing inanimate objects with human characteristics. Yet we also need to nurture our own unique identity and to keep at the lifelong task of knowing and understanding ourselves.

And Finally...Partnership and Porcupines

I'm reminded of a story recounted by Deborah Tannen in a discussion of our twin needs for involvement and independence. Porcupines, trying to get through a cold winter, "huddle together for warmth, but their sharp quills prick each other, so they pull away. But then they get cold. They have to keep adjusting their closeness and distance to keep from freezing and from getting pricked by their fellow porcupines—the source of both comfort and pain."

I live and work with other porcupines. They sometimes prick me, and I sometimes prick them. Sometimes I need to be pricked. And always I need them.

Here's to you and the other porcupines in your life.

May you, may we, keep learning how to live and work together,

partners in what we've been given to do.

Notes

Introduction

p. 3. On the zone of proximal development, see Vygotsky's original formulation in his book Mind in Society: Development of Higher Psychological Processes (Cambridge, MA: Harvard University Press, 1978), p. 86.

On the zone of reflective capacity, see Tinsley and Lebak's article "Expanding the Zone of Reflective Capacity: Taking Separate Journeys Together," available at http://journals.library.wisc.edu/index.php/networks/issue/view/32.

p. 6. Barry Oshry's definition of partnership is from his book Seeing Systems: Unlocking the Mysteries of Organizational Life (San Francisco, CA: Berrett-Koehler, 2007), p. 85.

p. 9. Oshry's description of Tops, Middles, and Bottoms is from his article "Total System Power: Developers, Fixers, Integrators, and Validators," available at http://www.powerandsystems.com/resources-a-thought-starters/articles.html.

Chapter 1

pp. 16-18. Peter Elbow's explanation of the believing and doubting games is the subject of the appendix essay in his book Writing Without Teachers (New York, NY: Oxford University Press, 1973).

p. 24. The "itch for closure" (Elbow, p. 177). If "you need answers" (Elbow, p. 178).

p. 24 "Being uncomfortable with uncertainty" is the title of Margaret Wheatley's epilogue in her book Leadership and the New Science: Learning about Organization from an Orderly Universe (San Francisco, CA: Berrett-Koehler, 1994), p. 149.

"Too often, seeking consensus . . ." (Edwin E. Olson and Glenda H. Eoyang, Facilitating Organization Change: Lessons from Complexity Science. San Francisco, CA: Jossey-Bass/Pfeiffer, 2001), p. 85.

p. 26. The film Meek's Cutoff was released by Oscilloscope Pictures in 2011. It was written by Jon Raymond; directed by Kelly Reichardt; and produced by Neil Kopp, Elizabeth Cuthrell, and David Uruttia.

Chapter 2

p. 33. John Wooden

p. 37. The guiding question as "container" (Olson and Eoyang, p. 11).

p. 38. Sam Kaner's distinction between divergent and convergent thinking is from his book Facilitator's Guide to Participatory Decision-Making (Gabriola Island, BC: New Society, 1996), pp. 6-20.

p. 40. Sparkie Anderson

p. 43. "There is an incessant influx of novelty . . . ." Henry David Thoreau, The Illustrated Walden. Ed., J. Lyndon Shanley. (Princeton, NJ: Princeton University Press, 1973), p. 332.

Chapter 3

pp. 51-52. The Parable of the Talents is recounted in Mt. 25:14-31. The quotations here are from the Bible, New American Standard Version.

p. 54. Oshry, "Total System Power."

p. 56. "A good informant is one . . . ." James P. Spradley and David W. McCurdy, The Cultural Experience: Ethnography in Complex Society (Chicago, IL: SRA, 1972), p. 47.

p. 56. "management by wandering around." Tom Peters and Robert Waterman, In Search of Excellence: Lessons from America's Best-Run Companies (New York, NY: HarperCollins, 2004, 1982), p. 289.

p. 61. "orientational metaphors." George Lakoff and Mark Johnson, Metaphors We Live By. (Chicago, IL: University of Chicago Press, 1980), pp. 14-21.

pp. 62-63. "Report talk" and "rapport talk." Deborah Tannen, You Just Don't Understand, Women and Men in Conversation (New York, NY: William Morrow and Co., 1990), pp. 76-77.

pp. 65-66. The film Hoosiers was released by De Haven Productions in 1982. It was written by Angelo Pizzo and directed by David Anspaugh. Gene Hackman played Norman Dale.

Chapter 4

p. 73. Calling as "committing one's self to becoming a good carpenter . . . ." Robert N. Bellah et al., Habits of the Heart: Individualism and Commitment in American Life (Berkeley, CA: University of California Press, 1985), p. 69.

p. 76. "Becoming human is becoming individual." Clifford Geertz, The Interpretation of Cultures (New York, NY: Basic Books, 1973), p. 52.

pp. 76, 78. Thomas S. Kuhn explains his notions of paradigm, paradigm shift, and normal science in his book, The Structure of Scientific Revolutions (Chicago, IL: University of Chicago Press, 1970).

p. 83. Paulo Friere's notions about education are explained in his book, Pedagogy of the Oppressed (New York, NY: Continuum, 2000, 1970).

Chapter 5

p. 96. "Trust thyself . . . ." Ralph Waldo Emerson, from " Self Reliance." In The American Tradition in Literature, 4th ed. Ed. Sculley Bradley et al. (New York, NY: W.W. Norton, 1974) , p. 1108.

Chapter 6

pp. 115 ff. Carol Ritberger's four-color scheme is from her book, Managing People: What's Personality Got to Do with It? (Carlsbad, CA: Hay House, 2007).

Conclusion

pp. 134-135. W. Timothy Gallwey, The Inner Game of Tennis (New York, NY: Bantam Books, 1974).

pp. 135-136. "condescension toward children's minds and abilities . . . ." Kenneth Koch, Rose, Where Did You Get that Red? Teaching Great Poetry to Children (New York, NY: Vintage Books, 1973), p. 7.

"better than most of those in elementary-school textbooks . . . ." Koch, p., 6.

pp. 142-143. The film Cast Away was released by Twentieth Century Fox in 2000. It was written by William Broyles Jr. and directed by Robert Zemckis.

p. 143. Deborah Tannen's story about porcupines comes from her book, You Just Don't Understand, p. 17. She attributes the original example to the philosopher Schopenhauer.

Suggested Reading

Alexander, C., Ishikawa, S., & Silverstein, M. (1977). *A Pattern Language: Towns, Buildings, Construction.* New York: Oxford University Press.

Alexander, C. (1979). *The Timeless Way of Building.* New York: Oxford University Press.

Anderson, D., & Anderson, L. S. (2001). *Beyond Change Management: Advanced Strategies for Today's Transformational Leaders.* San Francisco: Jossey-Bass/Pfeiffer.

Anderson, L. S., & Anderson, D. (2001). *The Change Leader's Roadmap: How to Navigate Your Organization's Transformation.* San Francisco, Calif.: Jossey-Bass/Pfeiffer.

Baldwin, C. (1998). *Calling The Circle: The First and Future Culture* (Bantam trade pbk. ed.). New York: Bantam Books.

Linked: the New Science of Networks. Cambridge, Mass.: Perseus Pub.

Barber, M. (2008). *Instruction to Deliver: Fighting to Transform Britain's Public Services* (Rev. pbk. ed.). London: Methuen.

Blankstein, A. M. (2010). *Failure is Not an Option: 6 Principles for Making Student Success the Only Option* (2nd ed.). Thousand Oaks, Calif.: Corwin Press.

Block, P. (1993). *Stewardship: Choosing Service Over Self-Interest.* San Francisco: Berrett-Koehler Publishers.

Bodaken, B., & Fritz, R. (2006). *The Managerial Moment of Truth: The Essential Step in Helping People Improve Performance.* New York: Free Press.

Bolman, L. G., & Deal, T. E. (2001). *Leading With Soul an Uncommon Journey of Spirit* (New and rev. ed.). San Francisco: Jossey-Bass.

Bolman, L. G., & Deal, T. E. (2002). *Reframing the Path to School Leadership: a Guide for Teachers and Principals.* Thousand Oaks, Calif.: Corwin Press.

Bolman, L. G., & Deal, T. E. (2008). *Reframing Organizations: Artistry, Choice, and Leadership* (4. ed.). San Francisco, Calif.: Jossey-Bass.

Boyatzis, R. E., & McKee, A. (2005). *Resonant Leadership: Renewing Yourself and Connecting with Others Through Mindfulness, Hope, and Compassion.* Boston: Harvard Business School Press.

Brafman, O., & Brafman, R. (2008). *Sway: The Irresistible Pull of Irrational Behavior.* New York: Doubleday.

Buckingham, M., & Clifton, D. O. (2001). *Now, Discover Your Strengths.* New York: Free Press.

Bunker, B. B., & Alban, B. (1997). *Large Group Interventions: Engaging the Whole System For Rapid Change.* San Francisco: Jossey-Bass.

Bushe, G. R. (2009). *Clear Leadership: Sustaining Real Collaboration and Partnership at Work* (Rev. ed.). Mountain View, Calif.: Davies-Black Pub..

Byrd, J., & Brown, P. L. (2003). *The Innovation Equation: Building Creativity and Risk Taking in Your Organization.* San Francisco: Jossey-Bass.

Chopra, D. (1993). *Creating Affluence: Wealth Consciousness in the Field of All Possibilities.* San Rafael, Calif.: New World Library.

Chopra, D. (1994). *The Seven Spiritual Laws of Success: a Practical Guide to the Fulfillment of Your Dreams.* San Rafael, Calif.: Amber-Allen Pub.

Christensen, C. M., Horn, M. B., & Johnson, C. W. (2008). *Disrupting Class: How Disruptive Innovation Will Change the Way the World Learns.* New York: McGraw-Hill.

Cleary, T. F. (1988). *The Art of War.* Boston: Shambhala.

Collins, J. C., & Porras, J. I. (1994). *Built to Last: Successful Habits of Visionary Companies.* New York: HarperBusiness.

Collins, J. C. (2001). *Good to Great: Why Some Companies Make the Leap--and Others Don't.* New York, NY: HarperBusiness.

Collins, J. C., & Hansen, M. T. (2011). *Great by Choice: Uncertainty, Chaos, and Luck : Why Some Thrive Despite Them All*. New York, NY: HarperCollins Publishers.

Deal, T. E., & Peterson, K. D. (1999). *Shaping School Culture: The Heart of Leadership*. San Francisco: Jossey-Bass Publishers.

Dewey, J. (1997). *How We Think*. Mineola, N.Y.: Dover Publications.

Drucker, P. F. (1990). *Managing the Non-Profit Organization: Practices and Principles*. New York, N.Y.: HarperCollins.

Drucker, P. F. (2001). *The Essential Drucker: Selections from the Management Works of Peter F. Drucker*. New York: HarperBusiness.

Drucker, P. F., & Collins, J. C. (2008). *The Five Most Important Questions You Will Ever Ask About Your Organization* ([New ed.). New York: Leader to Leader Institute.

Eoyang, G. H. (2003). *Voices From the Field*. Circles Pine, Minn.: Human Systems Dynamics Institute.

Frankl, V. E. (1984). *Man's Search for Meaning: an Introduction to Logotherapy* (3rd ed.). New York: Simon & Schuster.

Fritz, R. (1999). *The Path of Least Resistance for Managers Designing Organizations to Succeed*. San Francisco, CA: Berrett-Koehler Publishers.

Fullan, M. (2008). *The Six Secrets of Change: What the Best Leaders Do to Help Their Organizations Survive and Thrive*. San Francisco: Jossey-Bass.

Fullan, M. (2010). *Motion Leadership: the Skinny on Becoming Change Savvy*. Thousand Oaks, Calif.: Corwin.

Gardner, H. (1993). *Multiple Intelligences: the Theory in Practice*. New York, NY: Basic Books.

Gardner, H. (2000). *The Disciplined Mind: Beyond Facts and Standardized Tests, the K-12 Education That Every Child Deserves* (New ed.). New York: Penguin Books.

Garrison, J. W. (1997). *Dewey and Eros: Wisdom and Desire in the Art of Teaching*. New York: Teachers College Press.

Gerber, M. E. (1995). *The E-Myth Revisited: Why Most Small Businesses Don't Work and What to Do About It*. New York: CollinsBusiness.

Gharajedaghi, J. (1999). *Systems Thinking Managing Chaos and Complexity : a Platform For Designing Business Architecture*. Boston, Mass.: Butterworth-Heinemann.

Gladwell, M. (2005). *Blink: the Power of Thinking Without Thinking*. New York: Little, Brown and Co.

Gladwell, M. (2008). *Outliers: the Story of Success*. New York: Little, Brown and Co.

Goleman, D. (1998). *Working With Emotional Intelligence*. New York: Bantam Books.

Griffin, D. (2002). *The Emergence of Leadership: Linking Self-Organization and Ethics*. London: Routledge.

Hawken, P., Lovins, A. B., & Lovins, L. H. (1999). *Natural Capitalism: Creating the Next Industrial Revolution*. Boston: Little, Brown and Co.

Heath, C., & Heath, D. (2010). *Switch: How to Change Things When Change is Hard*. New York: Broadway Books.

Heemsbergen, B. (2004). *The Leader's Brain: How Are You Using the Other 95%*. Victoria, B.C.: Trafford.

Herman, S. M. (2002). *Rewiring Organizations for the Networked Economy: Organizing, Managing, and Leading in the Information Age*. San Francisco: Jossey-Bass/Pfeiffer.

Hesselbein, F., & Cohen, P. M. (1999). *Leader to Leader Enduring Insights on Leadership From the Drucker Foundation's Award-Winning Journal*. San Francisco: Jossey-Bass.

Holland, J. H. (1995). *Hidden Order: How Adaptation Builds Complexity.* Reading, Mass.: Addison-Wesley.

Holman, P., Devane, T., & Cady, S. (2007). *The Change Handbook: the Definitive Resource on Today's Best Methods for Engaging Whole Systems (2nd ed.).* San Francisco: Berrett-Koehler.

Hopcke, R. H. (1997). *There Are No Accidents: Synchronicity and the Stories of Our Lives.* New York: Riverhead Books.

Jenkins, L. (2008). *From Systems Thinking to Systemic Action: 48 Key Questions to Guide the Journey.* Lanham, Md.: Rowman & Littlefield Education.

Johnson, S. (2001). *Emergence: the Connected Lives of Ants, Brains, Cities, and Software.* New York: Scribner.

Kahane, A. (2004). *Solving Tough Problems: an Open Way of Talking, Listening, and Creating New Realities.* San Francisco: Berrett-Koehler.

Kaner, S. (2006). *Facilitator's Guide to Participatory Decision-Making (2nd ed.).* San Francisco, Calif.: Jossey-Bass.

Kanter, R. M. (2001). *Evolve!: Succeeding in the Digital Culture of Tomorrow.* Boston, Mass.: Harvard Business School Press.

Kaplan, R. S., & Norton, D. P. (2004). *Strategy Maps: Converting Intangible Assets Into Tangible Outcomes.* Boston: Harvard Business School Press.

Kauffman, S. A. (1995). *At Home in the Universe: the Search for Laws of Self-Organization and Complexity.* New York: Oxford University Press.

Kaufman, B. N. (1991). *Happiness is a Choice.* New York: Fawcett Columbine.

Keel, T. (2007). *Intuitive Leadership: Embracing a Paradigm of Narrative, Metaphor, and Chaos.* Grand Rapids, Mich.: Baker Books.

Kegan, R., & Lahey, L. L. (2001). *How the Way We Talk Can Change the Way We Work: Seven Languages for Transformation.* San Francisco: Jossey-Bass.

Kotter, J. P. (1996). *Leading Change*. Boston, Mass.: Harvard Business School Press.

Kouzes, J. M., & Posner, B. Z. (1999). *Encouraging the Heart: a Leader's Guide to Rewarding and Recognizing Others*. San Francisco, Calif.: Jossey-Bass.

Kouzes, J. M., & Posner, B. Z. (2010). *The Truth about Leadership: the No-fads, Heart-of-the-Matter Facts You Need to Know*. San Francisco, CA: Jossey-Bass.

Lakoff, G., & Johnson, M. (1980). *Metaphors We Live By*. Chicago: University of Chicago Press.

Lambert, L. (1998). *Building Leadership Capacity in Schools*. Alexandria, Va.: Association for Supervision and Curriculum Development.

Lee, G., & Lee, D. (2006). *Courage: the Backbone of Leadership*. San Francisco, CA: Jossey-Bass.

Lencioni, P. (2000). *The Four Obsessions of an Extraordinary Executive: a Leadership Fable*. San Francisco: Jossey-Bass.

Lencioni, P. (2002). *The Five Dysfunctions of a Team: a Leadership Fable*. San Francisco: Jossey-Bass.

Lencioni, P. (2006). *Silos, Politics, and Turf Wars: a Leadership Fable About Destroying the Barriers That Turn Colleagues Into Competitors*. San Francisco, CA: Jossey-Bass.

Loehr, J. E., & Schwartz, T. (2003). *The Power of Full Engagement: Managing Energy, Not Time, Is the Key to High Performance and Personal Renewal*. New York: Free Press.

Luft, J. (1984). *Group Processes: an Introduction to Group Dynamics (3rd ed.)*. Palo Alto: Mayfield Pub. Co.

Maeda, J. (2006). *The Laws of Simplicity*. Cambridge, Mass.: MIT Press.

Markham, D. J. (1999). *Spirit Linking Leadership: Working Through Resistance to Organizational Change*. New York: Paulist Press.

Massarik, F., & Carpenter, M. (2002). *Organization Development and Consulting: Perspectives and Foundations.* San Francisco: Jossey-Bass/Pfeiffer.

Maxwell, J. C. (1998). *The 21 Irrefutable Laws of Leadership: Follow Them and People Will Follow You.* Nashville, Tenn.: Thomas Nelson Publishers.

Maxwell, J. C. (2005). *The 360 [degree symbol] Leader: Developing Your Influence From Anywhere in the Oganization.* Nashville: Nelson Business.

McLuhan, T. C., & McLuhan, T. C. (1994). *The Way of the Earth: Encounters With Nature in Ancient and Contemporary Thought.* New York: Simon & Schuster.

Mintzberg, H. (1994). *The Rise and Fall of Strategic Planning: Reconceiving Roles for Planning, Plans, Planners.* New York: Free Press.

Mintzberg, H., Ahlstrand, B. W., & Lampel, J. (1998). *Strategy Safari: a Guided Tour Through the Wilds of Strategic Management.* New York: Free Press.

Mintzberg, H. (2009). *Managing.* San Francisco: Berrett-Koehler Publishers.

Muhammad, A., & Dufour, R. (2009). *Transforming School Culture: How to Overcome Staff Division.* Bloomington, IN: Solution Tree Press.

Nelson, J. (2001). *The Art of Focused Conversation for Schools: Over 100 Ways to Guide Clear Thinking and Promote Learning.* Gabriola Island, B.C.: New Society Publishers.

Oshry, B. (1994). *In the Middle.* Boston, MA: Power & Systems.

Oshry, B. (2007). *Seeing Systems: Unlocking the Mysteries of Organizational Life (2nd ed.).* San Francisco: Berrett-Koehler Publishers.

Owen, H. (1999). *The Spirit of Leadership: Liberating the Leader in Each of Us.* San Francisco, Calif.: Berrett-Koehler.

Patterson, K. (2002). *Crucial Conversations: Tools for Talking When Stakes Are High.* New York: McGraw-Hill.

Pink, D. H. (2002). *Free Agent Nation: the Future of Working for Yourself ([New ed.).* New York: Warner Books.

Pink, D. H. (2005). *A Whole New Mind: Moving From the Information Age to the Conceptual Age.* New York: Riverhead Books.

Pompa, L. (1971). *Vico's Theory of the Causes of Historical Change.* Kent Tunbridge Wells, Kent: Institute for Cultural Research.

Reeves, D. B. (2009). *Leading Change in Your School: How to Conquer Myths, Build Commitment, and Get Results.* Alexandria, Va.: Association for Supervision and Curriculum Development.

Ritberger, C. (2006). *Love-- What's Personality Got to Do With It?: Working at Love to Make Love Work.* Carlsbad, Calif.: Hay House.

Ritberger, C. (2007). *Managing People--: What's Personality Got to Do With It?.* Carlsbad, Calif.: Hay House.

Robert, M. (1998). *Strategy Pure and Simple II: How Winning Companies Dominate Their Competitors (Rev. ed.).* New York: McGraw Hill.

Robinson, A. G., & Stern, S. (1997). *Corporate Creativity: How Innovation and Improvement Actually Happen.* San Francisco: Berrett-Koehler Publishers.

Saccone, S. (2009). *Relational Intelligence: How Leaders Can Expand Their Influence Through a New Way of Being Smart.* San Francisco: Jossey-Bass.

Schein, E. H. (1999). *Process Consultation Revisited: Building the Helping Relationship.* Reading, Mass.: Addison-Wesley.

Schlechty, P. C. (2009). *Leading for Learning: How to Transform Schools Into Learning Organizations.* San Francisco, Calif.: Jossey-Bass.

Schuster, J. P., Carpenter, J., & Kane, M. P. (1996). *The Power of Open Book Management: Releasing the True Potential of People's Mind, Heart, and Hands.* New York: John Wiley.

Schwartz, T., Gomes, J., & McCarthy, C. (2010). *The Way We're Working Isn't Working: the Four Forgotten Needs That Energize Great Performance.* New York: Free Press.

Senge, P. M. (1990). *The Fifth Discipline: the Art and Practice of the Learning Organization.* New York: Doubleday/Currency.

Senge, P. M. (2000). *Schools That Learn: a Fifth Discipline Fieldbook for Educators, Parents, and Everyone Who Cares About Education.* New York: Doubleday.

Sergiovanni, T. J. (1996). *Leadership for the Schoolhouse: How is it Different? : Why Is it Important?.* San Francisco: Jossey-Bass Publishers.

Shaw, P. (2002). *Changing Conversations in Organizations: a Complexity Approach to Change.* London: Routledge.

Singleton, G. E., & Linton, C. (2006). *Courageous Conversations About Race: a Field Guide for Achieving Equity in Schools.* Thousand Oaks, Calif.: Corwin Press.

Smith, K. K., & Berg, D. N. (1987). *Paradoxes of Group Life: Understanding Conflict, Paralysis, and Movement in Group Dynamics.* San Francisco: Jossey-Bass.

Spencer, L. J. (1989). *Winning Through Participation: Meeting the Challenge of Corporate Change With the Technology of Participation.* Dubuque, Iowa: Kendall/Hunt Pub. Co.

Stacey, R. D. (1996). *Complexity and Creativity in Organizations.* San Francisco: Berrett-Koehler Publishers.

Stacey, R. D. (2001). *Complex Responsive Processes in Organizations: Learning and Knowledge Creation.* London: Routledge.

Stanfield, B. (2000). *The Art of Focused Conversation: 100 Ways to Access Group Wisdom in the Workplace.* Gabriola Island, B.C.: New Society Publishers.

Stanfield, B. (2002). *The Workshop Book: From Individual Creativity to Group Action.* Gabriola, B.C.: New Society Publishers.

Streatfield, P. J. (2001). *The Paradox of Control in Organizations.* London: Routledge.

Taleb, N. (2007). *The Black Swan: the Impact of the Highly Improbable.* New York: Random House.

Tolle, E. (2006). *A New Earth: Awakening to Your Life's Purpose.* New York: Plume.

Wagner, T. (2008). *The Global Achievement Gap: Why Even our Best Schools Don't Teach the New Survival Skills Our Children Need--and What We Can Do About It.* New York: Basic Books.

Watkins, J. M., & Mohr, B. J. (2001). *Appreciative Inquiry: Change at the Speed of Imagination.* San Francisco, Calif.: Jossey-Bass/Pfeiffer.

Weaver, R. G., & Farrell, J. D. (1997). *Managers as Facilitators: a Practical Guide to Getting Work Done in a Changing Workplace.* San Francisco: Berrett-Koehler.

Weick, K. E., & Sutcliffe, K. M. (2001). *Managing the Unexpected: Assuring High Performance in an Age of Complexity.* San Francisco: Jossey-Bass.

Wheatley, M. J., & Rogers, M. (1996). *A Simpler Way.* San Francisco: Berrett-Koehler Publishers.

Wheatley, M. J. (2002). *Turning to One Another: Simple Conversations to Restore Hope to the Future.* San Francisco, CA: Berrett-Koehler Publishers.

Made in the USA
Lexington, KY
26 June 2012